Johnny Cash
IS A FRIEND OF MINE

By

Henry Vaccaro

Table of Contents

Dedication

To My Late Mother Rosemarie Huhn Vaccaro and Father Dr. Sebastian P. Vaccaro MD

For My Daughter Toni, you are always an inspiration in kindness strength and beauty

For My Son Henry your creativity and ingenuity are wonderful gifts you share with us all, Thank you for your hard work in putting this book together

For My Son in Law and Daughter in Law Mark Bahary and Sheri Vaccaro

For My Grandchildren Alex John Bahary, Henry V. Vaccaro III and Lola Marie Vaccaro you are all true Blessings

In Memory of my Dear Sister Roe, you are with us always, and for my Niece

To Brother Sebastian and Sister Fran and for there children; Sammy and Olivia, Michael and Allison

To Sandy Thank you for being there

Thank you to my Nephew Keith Lowy and his family

Thank you to the Piancione Family for all the years filled with great Italian food

Thank you to Andy Papiccio for the photos from our Kramer Guitar days

Thank you to Mark Sisom of Sisom Design for the fine book cover and graphic design services

Thank you to JR. Stanton for your computer assistance

Thank you to Sunny Zebe for your assistance in formatting and proofing these pages

Thank you to our adopted rock star John Eddie for being Henry Jr.'s big brother

Car One to Base ....(Base to Car One) for you Ms. Helen and Barbara Hamilton

Thank You Mike Black, Robert Siliato, Debra L. Rothenberg, Angel Kames and Dave Gamble for the wonderful photos

In Memory of my Dear Friend Saul Rubin and for his children Dean, Bari and Betsy

In Memory of my Dear Friend Marshall Grant

In Memory of my Dear Friend Gene Nieto & for his children Gene, Jr., Suzanne, Patty and Chris

In Memory of Corp. Albert Vaccaro KIA in the Philippines and All who fought and died for our Country

In Memory of The Great, Mayor Frank Fiorentino and to his family

Thank You to Lou Robin and his wife Karen of Artist Consultants and The Estate Of Johnny Cash, John Carter Cash, Tara Cash, Cindy Cash, Kathy Cash, Rosanne Cash and The Estate of June Carter Cash, Carlene Carter, the Late Rosie Carter and Tiffany Lowe

Thank you to Bill Miller and his wife Shannon for keeping Johnny's Legacy with us

To all the musicians that have graced the stage with John, starting with Luther Perkins, Marshall Grant and W. S. Holland and all those that followed

In Memory of Mother Maybelle, Anita Carter and Helen Carter

In Memory of John's sister Reba Hancock and for her daughter Kelly

A very special Thank You to Bob Wootton who has been like a brother to me since we first met in 1977, Bob and I have been through a lot together and I treasure his friendship, to his wife Vicki and beautiful girls Scarlett and Montana

And of course Thank You to Johnny and June

Foreword

Johnny Cash is my idol and has been since I first heard that deep voice and boom chick-a-boom sound when I was a kid in 1956. Johnny Cash became my lifelong friend for over 30 years until his death. His family honored me by making me an honorary pallbearer at his funeral. Not a day goes by that I don't think of him and the fabulous hours we spent together. None of this would have happened if it were not for my friendship with Bob Wootton as Bob invited me to tag along on so many ventures with John from hanging out backstage to rides all over the country on JC UNIT ONE. I would not trade one minute of a ride on J C UNIT ONE for a ride on AIR FORCE ONE that's how special and blessed my life has been after befriending one JR Cash.

As I began telling stories about Johnny Cash to anyone that would listen, people would always say "Boy you should write a book." Well thank God over the years I always brought a camera with me on these adventures and kept notes, plus at my age now 72, my memory is still sharp. Several years ago or whenever things were slow in my business my son, Henry, Jr. would have me sit down in front of a small camera and talk. Pretty soon we chronicled over 20 stories so I felt it was time for this book. I am not a professional writer by any stretch of the imagination. The more I thought about it the better I felt about telling my stories in my own voice and hand. I decided that I didn't need any professional with fancy words just plain simple language the way I speak every day so that common folk, you the real Johnny Cash fans could relate.

These little stories are true, some of which have never been told before and in each instance I try to show a photo relating to that particular story. Some of these stories show the compassion and caring that this truly great man had for his fellow man. Some stories are funny, some sad but they are factual to the best of my memory. Most of all I hope you will get to see a side of Johnny Cash that few people have known.

Chapter 1
Admit Backstage

It was the summer of 1957 when I first discovered Johnny Cash. I was sixteen years old, going to be seventeen that fall, and my father had bought me a brand new car, a beautiful red and white Corvette as a birthday present. All I could do was admire it, as I didn't yet have a license. Instead, I'd just drive it up and down the driveway, and wash and polish it almost every day. I often parked

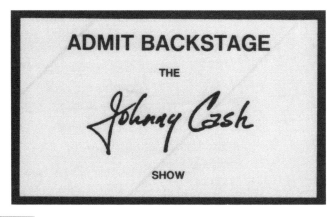

Me at the Age of 17

the car under the porte-cochere at our home; that way I could sit in it and listen to Johnny Cash on the record player blasting from inside the house. I had recently found a record of his—"Hot and Blue Guitar," one of his early Sun albums—and I think I listened to it over and over until it was time for me to get out of the car and wash up for dinner. I loved the early versions of "Folsom Prison Blues," "The Wreck of Old '97," the slowed down version of "Picking Time" and "Supper Time," and I was absolutely mesmerized by the deep honky-tonk sound and by his incredible voice. I then ordered a 45 rpm record, Johnny Cash's "The Ways of a Woman in Love," as no music stores in my area carried the Sun label. This became my favorite Johnny Cash song, and man, did I wear that thing out. I mean, I was in love with my girlfriend Diane at the time (whom I later married), but that record completely captivated me; it said it all.

The 50s: those were the years of rock and roll, and where I lived in Asbury Park, New Jersey; we hardly ever heard country music. In fact, you'd be called a hillbilly if you even listened to it. Specifically, the year was 1958 and I just started college, I was a freshman at Villanova University, and all of a sudden on the air I heard, "I Walk the Line." I knew it had come out earlier, but it was finally catching on in the north east and boy I just loved that record.

The next year my father passed away at age 51 of a massive heart attack. He was a medical doctor who literally worked himself to death. He was a general practitioner who firmly believed in and practiced his Hippocratic Oath, so his office was open seven days a week, and he made house calls every night. My dad, Sebastian P. Vaccaro, MD, had even been knighted for his humanitarian deeds by Pope John XXIII in a ceremony held at the Berkeley Carteret Hotel in Asbury Park. While he was still dressed in his tuxedo, he made several house calls after the

My Dad the Town Doctor

ceremony, returning home well after midnight. Two nights later he passed away in his sleep. My life would never be the same; I quit college to be home with my mom and began to pursue my lifelong dream of doing construction work. I bought a used backhoe and started digging ditches, installing septic systems, putting in oil tanks and anything else to earn a living.

Eventually I formed my own construction company, got married to Diane when I was 20 years old, and all the while, kept on listening to Johnny Cash. I finally heard on the radio that he would be performing in Newark, New Jersey at a place called Symphony Hall, and boy, I knew I had to go see him. The year was 1965; I sat in the audience like I was in a trance. The next concert of his I went to was at Madison Square Garden, in New York City around 1968. The place was packed, and I later learned that Johnny Cash was the first performer to sell out this magnificent brand new venue and I had been there! What was amazing about that feat is the fact that there was no Ticketron or Ticketmaster, certainly no MTV. You only found out about the concert on the radio or in the newspaper, yet he sold over 18,000 seats.

In the '60s and '70s I was my general construction business grew to the point where we were building schools, hospitals and other public buildings. On the side I liked to make small investments; for instance, I was instrumental in starting a guitar manufacturing company, a little company named Kramer Guitar. It's funny how that investment came about. I'd started building an industrial park on land that I purchased in nearby Neptune, New Jersey. My goal every year was to try and construct another building and rent it out in order to derive a steady income stream.

Well, by 1975 I had five or six buildings, and I was approached by a realtor by the name of Banks Bromann and a young man named Dennis Berardi, who wanted to rent one of my buildings to start a guitar company. I was intrigued.

Berardi said, "We're going to turn the music world upside down!"

"What's so special about your guitar?" I asked. "We have a patent pending on a revolutionary new aluminum neck system that makes this guitar sound like no other," he said proudly."

Well I didn't know anything about guitars, but I checked it out and was impressed. I asked if I could borrow it for a day or two, as I might be interested in investing in the company if they were still looking for investors. Right away, Berardi said, "We sure are."

So I took the guitar home. At that time I had a construction superintendent named Bill Ryan, and he had a son, Billy Ryan, who was one of the hottest guitar players on the Jersey Shore. Billy had played guitar with Bruce Springsteen in the early years and so I asked Bill Sr. to let his son play this guitar for me. So young Billy gets back to me the next day and says, "Wow, this thing is incredible! It's got this great sound, and this great sustain. However, it needs to be tweaked a little. It's kind of heavy, but if you could clean it up I think you might have yourself a real winner." Based on that assessment I agreed to the possibility of making an investment subject to reviewing a business plan.

Meanwhile, Dennis Berardi introduced me to a fellow by the name of Phil Petillo. Phil was an expert luthier, someone who builds guitars and other wood instruments by hand. He had a small shop in his home in Ocean Township, the next town over. Phil's claim to fame at that time was that he made custom handmade acoustic guitars and also took care of Bruce Springsteen's guitars. Along with designer Gary Kramer, Phil helped design and create the early prototype versions of the Kramer aluminum neck guitar. The neck was designed using raw aircraft grade aluminum, which was then forged in a giant press at the Kaiser Aluminum Plant in Erie, Pennsylvania. The raw forging then came to the shop where wood inserts were added to the underside and a plastic phenolic fingerboard was then glued to the playing surface. These added elements were put into a vice type clamp to hold while

An Early Model Kramer Guitar

curing, and after a 24-hour wait the entire assembly would be put onto a lathe for cutting down to the final size. This was an involved process, but I was impressed with the final product. The early versions were all handcrafted by Phil, including cutting out the aluminum neck from raw stock, and developing the glue and the phenolic fingerboard. The fingerboard in itself was unique, for it was a hard plastic material similar to the material that telephones and bowling balls were made of at the time. Traditional fingerboards are usually made of rosewood or ebony, but this one was fast on your hands and would not wear out. Then Dennis introduced me to his two other partners, Peter LaPlaca, a former VP of Norlin Music Corporation which owned Gibson Guitar, and Gary Kramer, who helped invent the first aluminum neck guitar made by Travis Bean.

Stanley Clarke Has The Talent

Kramer Has The Instrument

It's an award winning combo! In fact Stanley Clarke is an award winner. He was down beat readers' choice for electric bass player of the year in the 1976 poll. And his choice in bass guitars is Kramer model 450 B. Take it from an expert: Kramer is a winner too.

Kramer Guitars

New Generation Guitars.

BKL INTERNATIONAL DISTRIBUTING, LTD • 1111 GREEN GROVE ROAD • NEPTUNE, NEW JERSEY 07753 • (201) 922-8600

Meanwhile Kramer Guitar Co. had purchased space at the NAMM (National Association of Music Merchants) trade show in Chicago, which was to be held at McCormick Convention Center, a 1,000,000 square foot Expo Center. By now Kramer had gotten its first endorser, Stanley Clarke, a well renowned bass player. Dennis felt that with Stanley Clarke on board, Kramer could achieve its sales projection of selling a hundred thousand dollars of product at the show. I told Dennis if he met that goal, I'd invest in the company. I believe the show lasted four or five days, starting on Wednesday and going through Sunday. The next thing I knew, I got a frantic phone call on Friday from Dennis Berardi saying, "Henry, Henry, you got to get out here; we are the hit of the show!" Well, I quickly got a ticket and flew out to Chicago.

The Kramer trade show Booth

The first thing that hit me was the size of the show; it was enormous, maybe 500,000 square feet in size or larger. I was impressed with the Kramer booth too, how professional it was. We sold over five hundred thousand dollars of guitars and basses at that show, and some dealers were paying cash in advance to be the first ones to get this new guitar with its aluminum neck. I said "Holy shit!" then upgraded my ticket and flew first class going home. I said to myself, *Damn I'm now in the manufacturing business. Big time.*

Dennis Berardi and Me at the Beginning Days of Kramer

So, I flew home and things were starting to get crazy at the Kramer factory. We had all these orders coming in, the factory was not even set up, and some dealers were even sending in *more* money to make sure that their order took priority. But in order to get started, Kaiser Aluminum Company required a $60,000 check to pay for the mold, so what do I do, I made out the check and sent it over.

Meanwhile Dennis had engaged a local machine shop in nearby Wall, New Jersey, to do all the required work on the necks. Since we were in a hurry to start making the product I arranged for a truck to go to the Kaiser plant in Erie, Pennsylvania to pick up the raw forgings and deliver them directly to the machine shop. The next day Dennis and I went over to the shop only to be told that they were backlogged and too busy, and for us to leave the necks in the corner and maybe in two or three weeks they could start. I said to Dennis, "We can't wait. We've got orders to fill. This will ruin our reputation and that's no way to start a new business." Dennis said, "So what do we do?" I told him "Hell, if we are going to be in business we have to do it the right way; we can't be held hostage by any machine shop. I'll get the money, and we'll buy our own machines." So, I went out and bought a machine shop—not a shop per se, but bought all the machines that a machine shop needed to run an operation: a lathe, vertical and horizontal milling machines, a drill press, buffing wheels, belt sanders, band saw, etc.

We brought these machines back to the factory building in my industrial park and set up shop. Well, in our haste to get into production we had purchased the wrong models for some of the machines, and to make a long story short, it would take two shifts to complete eight to ten

Bill Spies, Myself and My Son Henry Jr.

necks a day, I guess some would call that a learning curve; I would call it a stupid mistake at my expense, as I was the dope that rushed into this mess. Plus it was my money at risk.

The next problem I soon found out was we needed a tool and die maker, since each machine required special tooling to adapt it to a specific task. Dennis called the Bridgeport Milling Machine Company who recommended a freelance tool and die maker who lived in North Jersey not too far from our factory. We interviewed one Bill Spies, a German machinist of the finest order. He was hired on the spot. It was like he was sent from heaven, the perfect man for the job. This man was so talented that he could have made a watch out of a block of steel. Bill solved our problems in no time.

We traded in a couple of the wrong machines and got the correct ones using True Trace attachments, so the machines would automatically follow a pattern that Bill designed. Our production now increased from eight to ten necks in a double shift to eight to ten necks in an hour. So much has to be said for having the right man for the right job, along with the right equipment.

That's actually the *short* version of the story on how Kramer Guitar Company got its start. Kramer eventually took off and became one of the largest American manufacturers in the 1980s. It took off with uncontrolled growth. We eventually dropped the aluminum neck in favor of the more traditional wooden neck because we had just gotten Eddie Van Halen as our main endorser and he wanted a wooden neck, so to hell with the aluminum; we switched to wood. Eddie Van Halen was to Kramer what Babe Ruth was to the Yankees or Red Grange to Pro Football. I mean we went *big* time, from 500 guitars a year to over 70,000. Kramer also had an exclusive deal to use the patented Floyd Rose tremolo (the bar attached to the bridge of a guitar that when pushed down tends to release the tension on the strings and create a wah-wah sound that heavy metal players like) which also helped to propel sales.

So that's my entry into the guitar business, and the whole reason I'm mentioning that fact is because at my first formal meeting with Johnny Cash, I introduced myself as being in the guitar business because I wanted to have something in common with him, even though my main business was building and construction.

I first met Johnny in August 1973, at a reception with about a hundred other guests after a show he performed at the Garden State Arts Center in Holmdel,

New Jersey. This was a benefit fundraiser, and other than a brief introduction I was unable to spend much time with him. As after making a token appearance and shaking hands with all the guests, he departed.

My first formal meeting with Johnny Cash was in 1977; I can't remember the exact date as I lose track of time, at my age (I'm 72, so I'm entitled to a pass). The meeting came about through my other company, the Henry V. Vaccaro Corporation, which was at that time building a 200-bed private hospital in Secaucus, New Jersey. This was a big hospital, maybe a thirty-million-dollar contract, and I was sitting in Dr. Paul Cavelli's office. He was the hospital founder, and he was discussing the possibility of having an outside firm manage the facility, a management company out of Nashville, Tennessee called Hospital Affiliates. Well, I'm always intrigued, and sitting in Cavelli's office reading this brochure about Hospital Affiliates, I saw that a member of the board of directors was Dr. Nat Winston, and that name rang a bell to me.

I had just finished reading Johnny's autobiography, *Man in Black*, a few weeks earlier, and in the book he attributes Nat Winston, a psychiatrist, with helping him get off his pill habit. So, I had Dr Cavalli in Secaucus contact Nat Winston, in Nashville, to arrange for me to have a personal meeting with Johnny Cash, who was soon going to perform at The Garden State Arts Center, out on the Garden State Parkway in New Jersey about 15 miles from my home. So thanks to Dr. Nat Winston, the arrangement was made. I met Johnny Cash and the start of a thirty-year phenomenal friendship began.

Like I said I introduced myself to Johnny, as being in the guitar business. I said "We have this new revolutionary guitar, and I'd love to show it to you." He said, "Well, we're staying at the Hilton Inn, near exit 105 of the Garden State Parkway, which happened to be about four miles from the Kramer guitar factory, why don't you come over tomorrow morning around 10 o'clock, and I'll introduce you to Bob Wootton, my lead guitar player, and Marshall Grant, my bass player."

Well, God does things in strange ways. I showed up at the Hilton Inn the next morning, and Marshall was expecting another guitar company, somebody who had previously contacted the House of Cash and had set up a meeting, but the guy didn't show up. I showed up and they thought I was the guy, so they let me in. I showed Bob and Marshall this new aluminum neck guitar and bass and they freaked out, so then I drove them to the factory four miles away.

And that night at the Garden State Arts Center, the entire Johnny Cash Show Band played aluminum neck Kramer Guitars. Marshall played a Kramer bass, Jerry Hensley, who I believe was a cousin of June's, played a Kramer guitar, and Bob Wootton, Johnny's lead guitar player and a member of the Tennessee Three, was on stage with a custom-made Kramer guitar. They all loved that new sound. So that's my introduction to the Johnny Cash Band. It really all started the prior night when I introduced myself to Johnny as being in the guitar business, so for the next two or three years, I would go to Johnny's concerts and hang out with Bob, who always saw to it that I had tickets and backstage passes.

Johnny and June thought of me as Henry the Guitar Maker, never knowing that I owned the whole guitar factory and had built and owned the buildings where it was housed. The guitar business was always stayed just a sideline.

That Very Night at the Garden State Arts Center Back in 1977,
The Johnny Cash Show Band Playing My Kramer Guitars

Chapter 2
Blessings in Bimini

Captain Jimmy Albury

In 1960, I had the privilege to fish with the immortal Captain Jimmy Albury on the fishing yacht *Falcon* based out of Weech's Dock in Bimini, Bahamas. Jimmy was a man's man, having served in the United States Navy during WWII and been a fisherman all his life. Before he died, Captain Jimmy was the only captain ever to boat three Blue Marlin over 700 pounds. After meeting him and getting to know him, I became addicted to both Captain Jimmy and to Bimini. As my fortunes grew, I always managed to have time to head south to my island in the sun, Bimini, two or three times a year. There I would entertain guests my company was doing business with, fish some of the best game fishing in the world, and recharge my batteries.

Bimini is one of the smaller out islands in the Bahamian chain, but it is perfectly situated as it's about 50 miles east of Miami and on the edge of the gulfstream. More records for big game fish have been set in Bimini than any other place in the world. While fishing with Captain Jimmy over a thirty-year period, I hooked (and lost) a giant blue-fin tuna well over a thousand pounds and caught a blue marlin that weighed 651 pounds. And on one trip I hooked and boated what was left of a giant blue-fin tuna that had been attacked and eaten alive by sharks. The head alone weighed 381 pounds, with all the meat gone exposing only the backbone and tail.

My Shark Eaten Blue-Fin Tuna

When I told all of that to Bob Wootton, Johnny Cash's guitar player and confidant, he yearned to go to Bimini.

Bob says, "Man I'd love to go fishing." So I invited Bob and Earl Poole Ball, Johnny's piano player, to Bimini in 1981. We all met in Miami at the airport as I flew in from New Jersey with my friends Saul Rubin and Gene Nieto, while Bob and Earl came by way of Nashville. After gathering up our luggage, I flagged down a cab and we all got in for the 25-minute ride to Watson's Island, halfway between Miami and Miami Beach. On this small island was Chalk's Seaplane Service, where I confirmed our reservations and dropped off our luggage. The time was around noon, and our flight wasn't scheduled to depart until 2:30, so we got back in the cab and headed to a little Italian restaurant that I knew of in Miami Beach for a good lunch before departing for Bimini. After stuffing ourselves on pasta and meatballs, we headed back to Watson Island to check in.

Earl, Bob, Me and My Dear Friend Saul Rubin

Chalk's Air Line at that time was the oldest airline in existence, having been founded by legendary aircraft pioneer A.B. "Pappy" Chalk in 1917. The airline flew mostly Grumman aircraft, whose models were named after water birds the likes of Widgeon, Goose, Super Goose, Mallard, and Albatross. Our flight was on a Super Goose, a World War II vintage plane that was upgraded to carry eight passengers and a pilot. If the plane was not overloaded, then an extra passenger could fit in the copilot's seat. Weight and balance were very important on these fragile planes; as you check in, in addition to putting your luggage on a scale, they ask your weight and write it down.

After boarding the plane on land which was a short 80 to 90 foot walk from the terminal, we watched the luggage being placed in the nose of the aircraft by an employee climbing up a small ladder. The pilot handed it to him piece by piece, and what didn't fit in the nose was put in the rear of the plane, right behind the passenger seats, and covered by a tarp. A funny thing happens after we taxied down a concrete ramp into the murky waters of Biscayne Bay, the pilot cranked up the wheels and the plane began floating like a boat. The only thing keeping us on an even keel was the two large pontoons, one at the end of each wing, which were now floating in the water.

As the pilot gunned the engines to full throttle, he suddenly started to throttle down and stopped. We looked nervously at each other. He took off his seatbelt, gets out of the cockpit turns around and said, "Hey, you two fat guys gotta move up here to balance the plane so we can take off." I looked around saw he was looking at Saul and me. A little embarrassed, we moved up toward the front of the aircraft, he then powered back up and we took off down Government Cut past all the docked tour ships and gradually lift off from the water on our way to the next adventure.

After a short uneventful flight of about 25 minutes, we circled the island of Bimini and started our landing approach from east to west with beautiful Bimini Bay underneath us. The pilot put the flaps down and headed for a safe landing in the crystal clear water. After the soft landing out comes the crank to jack down the wheels, that were stored in a compartment in the forward fuselage, this allows us to now taxi up the ramp adjacent to the Bahamian customs office.

Looking down at North Bimini

Soon after deplaning, we were all ushered into customs to obtain our entry permits. There was but only one taxi on the island, so we decided to walk fifteen minutes down King's Highway to the Bimini Big Game Fishing Club, followed by a native pushing a wheelbarrow filled with our suitcases.

This itself was an adventure. It is now 3:30 in the afternoon so we decided to kill the rest of the afternoon walking around the island and resting up for our first day of fishing, when we were all going after the, "Big One." It was the first week of June 1981 and giant tuna were still being caught just south of Bimini near the island of Cat Cay, on our first day out, Bob hooked a giant blue-fin tuna well over 700 pounds. The fight was on, but this time the tuna won, as it snapped Bob's line. That was all it took: Bob

Bob Hooking into a Giant Tuna

Bob, Me and Earl on the Bridge of The Falcon

was now hooked on big game fishing. (Folks, you really have to experience the thrill of a giant fish double or triple your weight as it hits your line—just imagine a depth charge exploding, that's the feeling you get when a giant blue- fin tuna attacks the bait.) We spent the rest of the week hunting for another giant, but to no avail; we caught plenty of smaller fish, but nothing over fifty or sixty pounds.

Back in those years I was a member of the Bimini Big Game Fishing Club, which had outstanding accommodations: a fifty-slip marina, and a great restaurant and lounge. After dinner there one night, we were entertained by a native named Ratti, who played the guitar and sang mostly Bahamian and island songs, to our delight. Two native songs that I learned and eventually could sing along to were "Conch Ain't Got no Bone" and "Shame and Scandal in the Family." After Ratti finished his set that night, Earl spotted an old upright piano in the far corner of the lounge area. When he sat down, he soon learned that it was out of tune, what was funny about this, is the piano had a date stenciled on the back which showed that the last time the piano was tuned was some 4 years prior which didn't matter to Earl that it was out of tune, as he sat down on the stool, because Earl could make any piano sound like a Steinway. Bob borrowed Ratti's guitar, tuned it, and then it was show time at the Big Game Fishing Club in old Bimini town. Bob and Earl put on a show that was worthy of a Carnegie Hall performance. They had the place jumping, and it wasn't long before all the folks, both natives and tourists, became enchanted and turned into instant Johnny Cash fans. The trip was a great success: not a lot of fish, but a lot of fun.

Bob, Me, Captain Jimmy and Earl
Having a grand Ole Time at The Big Game Club

On the way back to the States, Bob said, "Johnny would love this place. Why don't you invite him?" I told Bob that I was too embarrassed to ask him, and left it at that. But about six months later, I happened to be with John on his tour bus when he turned to me and said, "Bob told me about your trip to Bimini; I'd love to go there with you some time." That's all I needed to hear; Johnny checked his calendar and cleared a week the following summer.

So plans are made for the next trip to Bimini, Johnny Cash and all. I made the arrangements, including contacting Captain Jimmy for the boat and our housing accommodations and next thing I know we are ready to go. Now it's 1982 and I think it was probably July of 1982, we flew down to Bimini. Johnny, John Carter and Bob flew out of Nashville and I flew out of Newark with Gene Nieto. We all met at the Miami airport, We now had to trek over to Chalk's airbase, located on the small island between Miami and Miami Beach. We boarded a pre-World War II vintage Grumman Goose seaplane. It could only carry six passengers, three on a side on wooden benches leaning against the fuselage and facing each other; this was one of the older and smaller planes in Chalk's fleet. The flight to Bimini was bumpy, as the winds were starting to pick up. This meant that we would be landing in a choppy Bimini Bay. In fact, after landing and taxiing in the rough waters of the bay, the water began to come inside the fuselage of the plane, and we all had to raise our legs up to keep from getting wet.

Chalk's Seaplane

After we finally made it to the seaplane ramp and onto dry land, Johnny turned to me and said "Well Henry, that ride was a real adventure and kind of scary. Would you mind if we flew back on a Learjet?" What would you say, " Of course John, that's ok with me," as long as you insist. (I think another thing that scared Johnny was that he could see inside the cockpit, and noticed that the compass mounted near the controls had a piece of white adhesive tape affixed to it, marked in pen to note a course correction so that two degrees west was really eight degrees west.) So he called Nashville and spoke to his sister Reba, who arranged to have a Learjet pick us up at the airport in South Bimini five days later when our trip was over. What Johnny wanted, Johnny usually got.

There are three ways to get to North Bimini. You can take a seaplane and land in the bay directly in front of the hotels, clubs and marinas and be at customs in a matter of minutes, or you can take a land-based plane to the unpaved airport on South Bimini where after landing you can take an old taxi or pickup truck for the two-mile ride back to the dock. You can also walk, which I have done more than once when there was no taxi or truck at the airport, for the ride to the boat dock. Once at the dock, you pray that the water taxi is still running, that will eventually take you across the bay to customs on North Bimini. The third way is to take a boat from mainland Florida, directly to North Bimini or you can swim.

During our trip, we stayed at a private villa at Paradise Point on the north end of the island, and for the next four days we went out fishing. I had the most incredible time because I really got to spend some quality time, just to relax and be with Johnny Cash, it was, I mean, I felt like I was in heaven. What can be better than a diehard fan being friends with the number-one country star in the world?

We really hit it off, and Johnny told me stories of when he was a child and used to go fishing in a little pond with just a wooden stick, a string and a worm, there

Johnny, John Carter and Bob coming down from the Villa

Johnny Really Enjoying Our Trip

are no words to describe these moments, it was just like living a dream.

We had four good days of fishing and caught a lot of smaller fish: grouper, barracuda, amberjack, dolphin (mahi-mahi) and kingfish. I think the largest fish caught was a 70-pound Wahoo that John Carter got; his father later had it mounted for him.

At night, we would usually eat at the Big Game Club or a place called The Red Lion several hundred feet away, and get our exercise by walking the mile or so back to our villa at Paradise Point.

21

One night in particular after dinner at the Big Game Club, we were entertained again by Ratti, who played the guitar and sang. Johnny walked over to him and asked, "Do you mind if I tune your guitar?" With that, Johnny tuned the guitar and then sat down and played for everyone, no one asked him to, he just did it because he wanted too.

(Just picture Johnny in the movie *Walk the Line,* when he walked in to Columbia records and told them he was going to record in a prison—he didn't ask, he *told them*) That night Johnny sang because he wanted to, just look at the photo as I had never seen him so happy.

Johnny sang several songs and ended with "A Boy Named Sue." Soon after his first song, word spread like wildfire and people from all over descended on the club, they didn't want him to stop. When it was finally time to head back to our private villa, as we are walking, when John Carter berated his father

for using a cuss word in the song: "I'm the son-of-a-bitch that named you Sue" (in the record *Live at San Quentin* they bleeped that out). At that time, John Carter was a student at Goodpasture Christian School in Hendersonville, Tennessee and had been taught not to use curse words, so Johnny promised not to do it again. We then walked to our villa and retired for the night.

Johnny performing for us at The Bimini Big Game Club

The next day while we were out fishing, Johnny and I were topside when he started asking about my family and my background. I told him, "My dad was a doctor, and my mom was his nurse. My father used to take care of all the poor black patients in town that nobody wanted. He says tell me more and I told him, "My father had office hours seven days a week, made house calls every night till midnight, my mother by his side because he couldn't keep nurses; he would literally wear them out, my father's life was just dedicated to his patients, I mean he would see sometimes 80, 90 patients a day, he had office hours, even on Sunday." I also told Johnny that "Pope John XXIII, awarded him the Title of Knight Commander of Magisterial Grace In the Order of St. George in Carinthia for his humanitarian deeds and that a courier was sent over from Rome to bestow this honor." This all took place at this big testimonial dinner held at the Berkeley Carteret Hotel in the Asbury Park, New Jersey, on October 18, 1959. I proceeded to tell John "After the dinner, which lasted until around 11 PM while still in a tuxedo, my father made house calls until past midnight. I had gone back to Villanova University early the next morning, Fred Vaccaro, my father's cousin went with him to keep him company, and he recalled that one of his black patients had said, 'Here comes Jesus Christ, and he is dressed in a tuxedo.' Well my father was on cloud nine, and two nights later he went to sleep, and died in the middle of the night of a massive heart attack at 51 years old."

My Dad being Knighted at his Award Ceremony

Johnny was really spellbound by the story, and said to me, "How proud I should be of my Dad." After that we fished in thoughtful silence for a few more hours until it was time to head back to Bimini. All too soon, our fishing trip was over. Those 5 days went by so fast, Captain Jimmy arranged for the water taxi to pick us up at the dock located behind our villa, and to transport us across the bay to South Bimini where we hoped our Learjet would be waiting. After our water taxi ride from the villa to South Bimini we docked and looked around for some transportation to take us for the two mile jaunt to the airport. We found no one so I bribed a native who had a pickup truck to take us to the airport. Johnny and I sat in the cab with the driver and Gene, Bob and John Carter sat in the bed of the truck with our luggage.

Our Water Taxi Ride Over to South Bimini

Thank God, when we finally reached the airport we spotted this beautiful Learjet waiting for us. This was Bimini, so it wasn't over yet. Even though our plane was there, we couldn't board, as the immigration officer had gone back to North Bimini for lunch. So we were stuck in this airport building, I certainly can't call it a terminal; it was about 500 square feet with a counter and four or five chairs. It was hot as hell and no electricity or air conditioning. Now I understand why no one is here. You see there were no scheduled flights to and from this airport. Finally, our guy showed up, cleared us to leave, and into this jet we went.

Johnny and I Saying Goodbye to Bimini

This was my first experience on a private jet. Folks, believe me, this is the way to travel. It was like flying in a bullet: no sooner did we take off then it was time to land. Our flight took us directly to Atlanta and a private airport, where we never even cleared customs. Gene Nieto and I got off the plane as June, who'd flown up from Port Richey, got on, and they all headed to a show date in Little Rock, Arkansas. Gene then took a commercial flight home and I stayed in Atlanta for a few days to attend the NAMM music convention, where Kramer Guitar had a booth.

The following April, after that fishing trip, I was in my office when a Federal Express driver delivered a package from the House of Cash. I opened it and started to cry. While in Bimini, Johnny wore a small cross around his neck. It didn't mean anything to me, so I thought nothing of it, as I never wear any jewelry, crosses or anything. That Federal Express package contained that same small cross that Johnny had worn around his neck in Bimini.

Unbeknownst to me, he had given it to Captain Jimmy (who also made jewelry on the side) who then had it encased in a larger solid gold cross. On the back was this inscription: "For Henry, To The Memory of His Father, Sebastian Vaccaro From J. Cash, Easter 1983." That cross is now my most cherished possession, for it clearly shows the depth and character of this man that I came to know and love.

Chapter 3
Johnny Cash's America

"From the Nation's Capital to a Hospital in South Amboy, NJ"

The background to this next story started several years earlier. One of my very close friends, Gene Nieto, was the Director of South Amboy Hospital in the small community of South Amboy, New Jersey, located about a half hour drive south of New York City on the Raritan River. Gene also became friends with Johnny, as I would bring him along with me from time to time to see Johnny's shows. This story starts to unfold on Sunday June 20, 1982, at the Kennedy Center in Washington D.C., Johnny was performing for a television special called "Johnny Cash's America" to benefit the Lombardi Cancer Center. This was a two-hour special and the featured guests included the likes of Rodney Crowell, with a young Vince Gill playing rhythm guitar; John Prine, who sang about "Mister Peabody's Coal Train"; and Steve Goodman, who wrote and sang "City of New Orleans." This show was all about the America Johnny knew and loved, and this idea was shown in the songs he sang that night and the guests he chose and their song selections.

Steve Goodman and John Prine

Washington, D.C. was only a short four-hour drive from Asbury Park, so my two children, my daughter Toni and my son Henry Jr., piled into my car and off to D.C. we went. We planned to make this trip into a mini vacation, so on Friday the 18th of June we arrived in Washington and checked into the Howard Johnson Motor Inn across the street from the Watergate Apartments, within walking distance of the Kennedy Center. Johnny's sister Reba, who ran the House of Cash, had made our reservations and allowed us to use their corporate discount rate. Basically, all the performers

Rodney Crowell and Rosanne Cash

stayed at this hotel, and I recall talking to Rosanne in the lobby while she sat watching her children, who were still in baby carriages. She was married to Rodney Crowell at the time.

I also recall taking John Carter and my son Henry Jr. over to a magic store that I had found in the phone book called Al's Magic Shop located right in downtown Washington. The kids spent a good couple of hours there. And once the owner, Al Cohen, found out who John Carter's father was, boy, did we get the royal treatment. Not only did he show the kids magic tricks that they could buy, but being a magician himself, he put on a little show. We must have spent about a hundred bucks

Backstage Sharing some laughs

on all types of gimmicks, some of which John Carter later tried on his dad.

The next day was spent mostly at the Kennedy Center as day-long rehearsals took place. Toni and I actually sat in the orchestra pit of this vacant theater and watched the performers go through their paces, while the boys played on the floor backstage.

The Boys at Al's Magic Shop

Fast forward 22 Years later, my daughter Toni and I were backstage after a Marty Stuart concert and we were all talking about the good times hanging around with Johnny and June, when Marty piped up and said, "Do you remember those two heathens [Henry Jr. and John Carter] playing marbles on the floor backstage at the Kennedy Center? While we are breaking our chops rehearsing, they were laughing and playing on the floor."

Years later My Daughter Toni, Myself and Marty Stuart

The Two Heathens

During the rehearsals, Johnny was tenacious, and it seemed like he sang every song he ever recorded. The show featured the entire Johnny Cash Show Band with Bob Wootton on lead guitar; Marty Stuart on guitar, mandolin and fiddle; W S Holland on drums; Jack Hale Jr. and Bob Lewin on horns; Earl Poole Ball on piano; and Joe Allen on bass. The director pared down the songs from Johnny's list to fit within the strict time limits of the actual show, including weaving in the other artists and their repertoires.

By watching Johnny from such a close vantage point I could sense that he was in some kind of pain, although he would never admit it, as he was from the "old school." As it turned out, that prior winter, while fooling around in his fenced in game preserve back home, Johnny had been chased and kicked in the ribs by a pet ostrich. Directly across from the Cash home on Old Hickory Lake in Hendersonville, Tennessee where he had purchased a 60- or 70-acre parcel of land, had it fenced in, and made a game preserve there. At one time Johnny had deer, ostrich, pigs, goats, emu, rabbits, wild boar and who knows what else roaming around freely in this natural setting. He even built an authentic log cabin where he could hide out from the rest of the world. The cabin was later turned into Johnny's recording studio and used to record some of the American recordings; now it's been expanded and houses John Carter's recording studio.

Johnny's Cabin on His Wild Game Preserve

So after the ostrich attack and his subsequent fall, Johnny suffered several broken ribs, and a gash on his stomach and a deep cut on his knee. Johnny went to the hospital where they wrapped his ribs with tape, cleaned out and treated the wound's both on his stomach and his knee. They required many sutures, and he was told to stay off his feet and rest up until the wound's healed. Well, as luck would have it, Johnny injured the same knee about a week before the show and again it required sutures. Johnny knew better than the doctor and would not stay off his feet, besides he had a show to do. But being on his feet for such a long period of time during the rehearsal, his knee started to ache, Johnny being Johnny, he told no one. The next night, just before show time, he simply wrapped his knee and completed the two hour "Johnny Cash's America Special" without once giving the audience the least hint of his pain. After the show, the knee started to swell, but being the trouper that he was, he boarded the tour bus and off he was to the next venue, near Cherry Hill, New Jersey.

By this time, I had put the kids in my car and headed home. According to June, he was in a lot of pain by this point; the knee was really swelling up so she put ice on it. The next night, he had a sold-out show, and as the old saying goes, "the show must go on." Johnny performed that night in all kinds of pain as the knee was now infected. Early the next morning, I received a call from June telling me that John must get to a doctor as she thought the infection was getting worse. One of the stitches had popped open and the wound was seeping. June asked me what local doctor I would recommend, as the Hilton they were staying at was only a one-hour drive from my home.

Johnny always taking time for his fans

They were planning to leave the hotel to head to New York City and to rest up in their apartment, it would only have been a short detour to come to Asbury Park maybe a hour out of the way, and if I could find John a doctor. I thought about it for a moment and suggested since they were heading into the city, that their route would take them within three or four miles of Gene Nieto's hospital in South Amboy. What is ironic my firm The Henry V. Vaccaro Corp. built South Amboy Hospital ten years earlier and that's how my friendship with Nieto developed. Johnny and Gene were already friends from our fishing trips together, and June thought that was a great idea, as Johnny could get better treatment in the hospital. I immediately called

My Good Friend Gene Nieto and Johnny

Gene, told him the situation, and with his connections he arranged for the New Jersey State Police to intercept the Cash tour bus on the Turnpike near Sayreville, and escort it to the emergency entrance of South Amboy Hospital.

Gene had a full staff awaiting the arrival of their patient. Johnny hobbled out of the bus and was taken right inside for examination. Apparently, word spread like wildfire, that Johnny Cash was in the emergency room and the nurses were fighting to take his temperature and blood pressure. While in the hospital the doctor cut open the sutures, cleaned out the wound, stitched it back up and applied a dressing. Johnny was given antibiotics and sent on his way. South Amboy

29

is a small community, and the Johnny Cash visit was the biggest thing to hit the South Amboy area since the munitions explosion of 1950 at the pier that killed 27 people, or the commuter train that fell off the trestle at near by Woodbridge NJ, the following year, taking the lives of 51 passengers, including former New York Yankee second baseman George "Snuffy" Stirnweiss. As John was exiting the hospital getting ready to board his bus, a crowd of people was waiting to

wish him well and to see him off. The next day it was front page news in the local paper, and my friend Gene now walked around town with his chest puffed out.

Gene's hospital was a local, small facility while across the river sat two monster regional hospitals, Perth Amboy General Hospital with its 400 beds and JFK Hospital in Edison, a 500-bed

facility, so there was a rivalry between them and they all wondered why Johnny Cash had bypassed their magnificent facilities to wind up at lowly South Amboy Hospital. Little did they know that their fortunes were sealed by fate, the die had already been cast. And that's the way it was, when Johnny Cash visited his friend Gene Nieto and lit up the sleepy town of South Amboy New Jersey.

Gene proudly walking John out of his Hospital

30

Chapter 4

Murder in Coweta County

Johnny was making a movie in Georgia called *Murder in Coweta County*. Bob Wootton invited me down for ten days while the movie was being made.(Bob headed up the security for John on the movie set, and in one of the photos you can see him with a holster and pistol strapped on his right leg) This was the fall of 1982. I flew down to Atlanta; they had a car from the production company pick me up at the airport and take me to the backwoods of a little town called Griffin, Georgia, where the movie was being made. This was a made-for-TV movie of the week, the true story of a sheriff named Lamar Potts (played by Johnny Cash) and a land baron by the name of John Wallace (played by Andy

Roger Morton John's Bus Driver, Me and Bob

31

Griffith). John Wallace had killed a man and thought he could get away with it, as the only witness was a former slave. It was the first time in history of the South that a white man was convicted by the testimony of a black slave. It was really an interesting story.

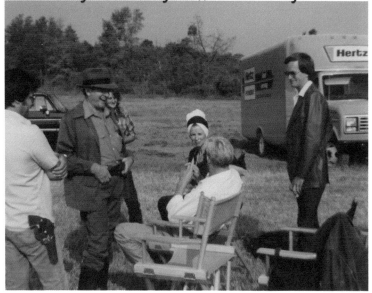

Bob, Johnny, June, Andy Griffith and Gary Baker on

June also had a part in the movie, as she played an old psychic woman named Mayhayley Lancaster. I got to see first hand how a movie is made. It was an experience that the average guy would die for. It was interesting to watch June come out of the makeup trailer dressed to perfection with the clothes of that period, right down to the colored contact lenses in her eyes to make them appear dark green. Another thing that stood out as I watched various scenes being shot was that when the director would yell cut, everyone would stop in place, and a production assistant would take a Polaroid photo of each actor, I was inquisitive and asked John why they did that? He told me, so that when the filming resumed they could compare and make sure the clothing, hair, and other features were exactly the same as when the director yelled cut. If the director yelled, "That's a wrap," it would mean that particular scene was over, and it would not have to be reshot; no Polaroid photo was required.

What also surprised me was the royal treatment everyone received on the set. Here we were in a swamp, hot as hell, several miles from a main highway, and a mile or so down a typical old Georgia clay road. On one hand it was dirty and dusty on the other hot and humid. Now picture that, right smack in the middle of this mess, sat a full-service food truck, the likes of which I had never seen. This was nothing like the food trucks you see around a construction site, but was actually a portable restaurant on wheels. I am not exaggerating when I say that sucker was 25- to 30-feet long with a complete kitchen, a full staff, and a gourmet chef.

Some of the dishes were already prepared but you could order anything from filet

Andy Griffith, Me and Johnny on set

mignon to sautéed veal. Adjacent to the truck was a large open dining tent filled with tables and chairs, and it's not too hard to guess where I hung out while Johnny or June were off shooting a scene. This entire food operation would follow the shooting schedule from one location to another and set up where required.

Looking at Johnny's cut brake lines

Something bizarre happened one night on the movie set: someone tried to sabotage a classic Ford police car that Johnny was supposed to drive down a steep winding road by slashing the brake line on the rear wheels. This was discovered by a mechanic early Monday morning on October 18, 1982. The gas tank of a different classic car had been filled with sugar, all in an attempt to mess up this movie. According to Johnny the motive was clear: "This movie we are shooting is very upsetting to a lot of folks here." It was, after all, the true story of the first white man in the south ever to be electrocuted on the testimony of a black man. Lt. Dean Ray of the Griffin, Georgia police department was also investigating two phone threats on Johnny's life—hence the heavy security, with Bob Wootton packing a pistol on his hip.

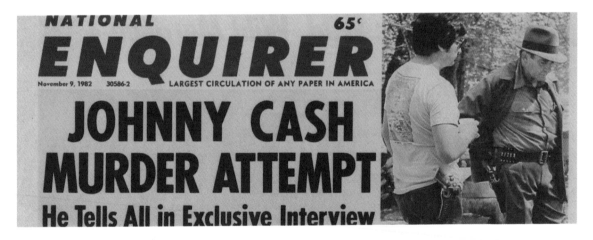

One day we went back in the swamp to film a scene and I'm on Johnny's tour bus JC Unit One, the bus also doubled as a dressing room, and a hide out where John could get a little rest and go over his lines. I'm alone on the bus with June while John was out shooting. She says well tell me a little bit about where you come from Henry, so I was telling her about my hometown and I had several photographs of Asbury Park New Jersey with me. I proceeded to tell her that it had been a fabulous seashore resort town from the 30s to the 50s, and then it started to deteriorate, like a lot of older seashore towns. The city had a stock of old wooden hotels that either burned down and never got replaced or were ruined by riots in the late 60s, and now the town was really struggling to get it's identity back.

Me Sitting on Johnny's Bus

As I told her about Asbury Park, I showed her a picture of an old hotel, the 450 room Berkeley Carteret, which I was in the process of buying. I also had a bid in to buy the entire beachfront, including the incredible convention center and magnificent theatre called the Paramount. June said, "I recall mama telling me something about playing in Asbury Park." (For folks that don't know this her mother was Maybelle Carter of the famous Carter family; the first real family of country music.) Back in the '40s, June told me, the Carter Family was scheduled to be on the cover of *Life* magazine in the first week of December, except something happened to change all that: the Japanese sneak attack on our naval base at Pearl Harbor, Hawaii, on

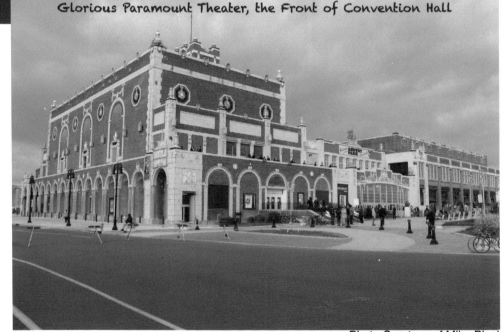

Glorious Paramount Theater, the Front of Convention Hall

Photo Courtesy of Mike Black

December 7th 1941. For some unknown reason that event pushed the Carter family right off of the cover—talk about bad timing. (*The Carter family never made the cover*)

But it was very interesting and informative just listening to June talk about her family and that rich country tradition and heritage, you felt that you had just gotten a lesson in the history of country music from a renowned professor.

June was really intrigued with the photos I showed her of Asbury Park. I was sitting down in the tour bus, which John had custom built several years earlier, and there was a little sitting area up front, with banquette seats facing each other, a table on the left side and two swivel chairs on the right. The area immediately to the rear of the sitting area was John's compartment, with access only through a private door.

34

It contained a black leather reclining chair, on the left side as you walked in, a television set above, and recording equipment built into a cabinet. The right side contained another banquette table, with double seats facing each other, and naturally the upholstery was black. At night the table would collapse and the seats would fold down and become Johnny's bed. This area also included a private bathroom trimmed with gold hardware. June and I were sitting in the forward area talking, when Johnny came on the bus to take a break from his shooting. He changed his sweaty shirt, grabbed a Coca-Cola from the refrigerator, sat down and wiped the perspiration off his forehead. All three of us were sitting in the forward area, and I'll never forget this, June turned to John and in her classic Virginia accent said, "Why John, look what Henry is wanting to buy." I showed him the pictures, he pointed to the theater and said "Well if you buy that, I want to open it up for you, and it won't cost you a penny. I want to be the first performer to play there after you get it."

I said, "John that would be great, but I can't accept that. It would be an honor to have you open that place up, but I want to pay you like everybody else pays you. However, if you want to take that money and invest it in the hotel, maybe we could do something." John said, "That sounds interesting; let me think about it."

The Magnificent Berkeley Carteret Hotel and Asbury Park Convention Hall

Photo Courtesy of Mike Black

And unbeknownst to me he called Nashville and asked his accountant, Gary Baker, to fly out to Griffin, Georgia the very next day. In an open field on the movie set, Johnny introduced me to Mr. Gary Baker, and explained my proposition to him and what I wanted to do. John asked him if he was available to fly to Asbury Park within the next couple of weeks and look at my hotel project. Gary responded that he would find the time.

Gary, as I recall, spent the night in Griffin and we had breakfast together the next morning. He was quite a guy, as he told me that he also represented Conway Twitty and helped set up Twitty City, an entertainment complex located across the street from the House of Cash on Johnny Cash Parkway in Hendersonville, Tennessee. Gary represented Waylon Jennings as well. And he had a strange hobby and passion for a pencil pusher: he drove stock cars in the NASCAR circuit. In fact, he had just crashed at Talladega and was on the mend when we met.

Anyway, we set up the arrangements for him to fly to New Jersey; his job was to inspect the hotel and review the documents and report back. Gary left to return to Nashville, and Johnny said to me, " if the project turns out to be as good as I said it would be, and Gary can confirm that, I think we got us a deal." He reached out his hand to shake mine, and that is how Johnny Cash became my first investor in the Berkeley Carteret Hotel. *(Gary did in fact come to Asbury Park reviewed the plans and feasibility study for the hotel and toured the beachfront area .It was upon his recommendation that John and June Carter Cash made an investment in the Berkeley Carteret Hotel restoration)*

BERKELEY-CARTERET ASSOCIATES LIMITED PARTNERSHIP

SIGNATURE PAGE
TO
AMENDED AND RESTATED
CERTIFICATE OF
LIMITED PARTNERSHIP

Signature(s) of Limited Partner(s)

Printed Name(s) of Limited Partner(s)

SIGNATURE(S) MUST BE ACKNOWLEDGED IN APPROPRIATE PLACE ON FOLLOWING PAGE(S)

Our Signed Partnership Agreement

36

Chapter 5
Johnny Cash Comes to Town

Photo Courtesy of Mike Black

On the morning of March 23, 1983 I was in my car on the way to Newark Airport to pick up Johnny Cash and bring him to Asbury Park, where we planned to spend the afternoon and then attend the City Council Meeting at 5:30 to meet Mayor Ray Kramer. The story really started three weeks earlier in Florida while I traveled with John on a tour through the state of Florida. June was ill and in the hospital, so Carlene took her place in the show. Also appearing in the Johnny Cash Show on that tour was Steve Goodman from Chicago who penned such hits as "The City of New Orleans," which was recorded by Johnny Cash , Willie Nelson and others, and "You Never Even Called Me by My Name." a song that became the trademark for David Alan Coe

June and Steve Goodman

Steve was suffering from leukemia and John wanted to help him. Steve first appeared as John's special guest the year before on the television special from the Kennedy Center in Washington D.C.

37

called Johnny Cash's America where he sang with John Prine and get this, a young Vince Gill is playing backup guitar on the show. Steve was an incredible talent and I really enjoyed spending time with him. He told me that his one last wish would be to have his beloved Chicago Cubs win the World Series, but he never got that wish. Sadly, he passed away the next year at age 36.

Johnny and June Eating Some of the Great Italian Food
I Would Often Bring Them

While sitting backstage with John, out of the clear blue sky he turned to me and said, "Henry, if I am going to be involved with you in Asbury Park, don't you think that I should be actually seen there?"

I was flabbergasted and said, "That would be great!"

"Okay, Reba will call you and set it up," said John.

(*Reba was John's sister and along with her daughter Kelly ran The House of Cash as John's office and museum.*)

Quite frankly, I forgot about the offer until one day, sure enough, Reba called and told me Johnny was coming to town. He'd be arriving at Newark Airport at 10:30 a.m. tomorrow March 23, 1983 can you pick him up, "Of course" I replied I left my office around 9 a.m. for the one-hour drive to Newark airport. While approaching the halfway marker on the Garden State Parkway, suddenly my secretary Helen's voice came over my Motorola two-way radio "Base to car one, base to car one" I pick up the microphone and said, "Car One to Base, what's going on Helen?" "Reba just called, Johnny who was in Port Richey Florida missed his flight to Newark, and would now be flying into LaGuardia at 1:15 instead. Curt, his limo driver, would be picking him up. I had little choice but to exit off the Parkway, turn around and head back to my office.

By the time I got back to my office it was around 11 o'clock, just time enough to locate one of my employees, Billy Garofolo, and ask him to drive me to LaGuardia. I arrived there just in time to greet John, who was coming down the walkway headed toward baggage claim. I waited as he picked up a small bag and we walked together to his limo. Curt opened the door and we both got in. John apologized for the mix up but said since he was in the city, this would give him the opportunity to make two stops: one to his dentist and the other to see Dick Asher over at Columbia Records. We headed to the dentist and I waited in the car; his visit only lasted about a half hour. Afterwards, we headed to CBS Headquarters at 51 West 52nd Street, also known as Black Rock. As John got out of the car he said, "Henry come on in with me; I want you to meet somebody."

So I followed Johnny Cash into this magnificent building to the office of Dick Asher, the somebody he wanted me to meet. As it turned out, Dick was a longtime friend and the president of Columbia Records. I was mesmerized to be introduced to this powerful and prominent man by Johnny, who invites me into Dick's office where I witness them discussing Johnny's new album. Johnny explained that we were headed to Asbury Park to check out the Berkeley Carteret Hotel as he has invested

M. Richard Asher
Deputy President, Chief Operating Officer
CBS/Records Group, CBS Inc.

President, CBS Records Division

CBS/Records Group
CBS Inc., 51 West 52 Street
New York, New York 10019

(212) 975-5955

with me in the hotel restoration project. Dick Asher told us he had fond memories of the old hotel and if we need another investor to call him up. This just shows the influence that Johnny wielded in the music industry. It was now getting late, around 5:30 p.m., and we were expected in Asbury Park at 6:30. Anyone who's ever tried to get out of New York City at rush hour knows that's impossible, but on our way we went.

We finally clear the Lincoln Tunnel and reached the New Jersey Turnpike around 7:30. I asked Curt to stop at the rest area so I could make a phone call to the Mayor and advise him of our late arrival. There was no way to reach the Mayor directly so I called the police department, which was located in the same building as the council chambers, and asked the captain on duty to please go next door and let the Mayor know we would be late. A lot of people in town were skeptical as to whether Johnny would even show up, and suspected the whole thing was a gimmick.

At 8:45, our big limo pulled up to city hall and out came this giant of a man: Johnny Cash all of 6'3, dressed in his trademark black outfit of Andrew Jackson boots laced to his knees, topped off with a black cowboy duster and a black cape with red lining. You would have thought that the Pope had just arrived. Despite our late arrival, not one person had left, and all immediately felt his presence. After meeting the Mayor and Council, Johnny spoke to all the folks. They were so moved that I was waiting for them to kneel down and kiss his ring. This all happened the day Johnny Cash came to town: March 23, 1983.

Johnny Certainly Made an Impression at the Asbury Park City Council Meeting

Asbury Park Press

Singer Johnny Cash (center) tours Convention Hall, Asbury Park, yesterday with Neptune builder Henry V. Vaccaro (left) and City Councilman Lorenzo Harris. Cash and Vaccaro want to redevelop the city's oceanfront property

Johnny Cash impressed by city renewal potential

By PATRICIA BATTLE
Press Staff Writer

ASBURY PARK — Country and western singer Johnny Cash says if he has anything to do with it, the city's Boardwalk will be restored to its former glory.

Cash visited the city yesterday for the first time since Neptune builder Henry V. Vaccaro unveiled plans to redevelop the Boardwalk, with Cash as an investor.

He said he is impressed with the potential for redevelopment he saw in the Boardwalk.

"It's given me a lift, I can tell you that," Cash said of his visit here.

"It's always bugged me to see people tearing down something old and beautiful," he said.

"I love the way all the old things are still here and intact," he said as he examined an old copper lantern on the roof of Convention Hall.

"The building materials — the iron, the copper, the velvet, the hardware — the whole thing is just magnificent."

Cash was brought to the city by Vacca-

Boardwalk back to the elegant status it held years ago.

Vaccaro and Cash are two of the four principals of A.P. Boardwalk Associates Inc., which bid $2,650,000 last month for the mile-long strip of land extending from Ocean Grove to Loch Arbour.

But the City Council was forced to reject the bid after two other prospective bidders and a city landlord took the city to court challenging the validity of the sale.

Superior Court Judge Patrick J. McGann Jr. earlier this month barred the council from selling the property to Vaccaro's corporation, labeling the bid specifications for the project "intrinsically invalid."

However, Vaccaro remains undaunted in his quest to buy the Boardwalk.

"I feel it's my destiny to straighten out this city," Vaccaro said last night. "I want to do it for my father. All I want is a chance to restore this city to the cultural elegance it deserves."

And Cash wants to help him do it.

"I had heard so much about Asbury Park and Henry's dreams for it, I had to see it," he said. "I can bring my little boy

Cash said his 13-year-old son, John Carter Cash, "would like to see a video center, and my wife would like an antique store" included in the redevelopment plans.

He explained he and his wife, June, have collected antiques for the past 15 years. His home in Hendersonville, Tenn., is full of antique furnishings, he added.

"Oh, boy!" he exclaimed as he walked into Convention Hall. "Isn't this beautiful. A building like this is a treasure. Carnegie Hall has nothing on this place. I'd rather play here ..."

The architecture and style of the buildings he visited last night interested him more than anything else, he said.

Vaccaro, president of the corporation, said he plans to restore the Paramount Theatre in Convention Hall as a cultural center and Cash has pledged to perform the opening show.

Cash stood on the stage of the Paramount and recited a few lines from Shakespeare's "Julius Caesar" to the vacant house.

Chapter 6 The Betty Ford Clinic

In late November of 1983, I got a phone call from Reba, Johnny's sister. I was on a construction project down in South Jersey, and Reba said, "Henry can we ask a favor of you?" I said, "Of course," and she said, "Johnny's very sick. He just landed in New York from London and June stayed behind to be with her daughter Carlene. John's got to get to a hospital right away, but he will not go to a hospital in New York, so we have to get him to Nashville." Carlene, at the time, was married to Nick Lowe, the British rock star. Carlene was doing an off-Broadway show in London, near Piccadilly Circus, so June wanted to stay and spend some quality time with her.

Reba proceeded to tell me that Johnny was in New York, in their apartment with John Carter. "I have a Learjet coming for him, and the plane will be coming into Teterboro Airport. Is there any way you could pick John up at the apartment and get him to the airport, and is it possible for John Carter to stay with you?"

"Absolutely," I said. I was way down in South Jersey, but I shot up to New York on the Turnpike; it probably took me an hour and a half. I picked John up at his apartment and he told me he had been bitten by a spider, and had developed a bad staph infection as a result. The local doctor wanted to admit him right away to a hospital in New York, but he refused: "I'm not going to any hospital in New York; I got to get home." So I drove him over to Teterboro where I put him on a plane, and John Carter then came back home with me.

That just shows the trust they had in me to leave their only son with my family in their time of need. I later found out that this was the first time that John Carter Cash had gone anywhere without a bodyguard being present.

At that time I was divorced, and John Carter, who was friends with my son Henry Jr., stayed in Short Hills, New Jersey, where my ex-wife was living with my two children. John Carter even went to school with my son; he ended up staying two weeks with Henry Jr. You can just imagine the school kids when they went home and told their parents who was sitting in class with them. After John flew back to Nashville, he was quickly admitted to Baptist Hospital where among other health problems the doctors discovered that he had a bleeding ulcer that required immediate surgery. He lost three units of blood, and surgery was performed even though he had a staph infection.

Our Sons, Henry Jr and John Carter

He came out of surgery okay, but almost instantly he was addicted to the morphine and other prescription drugs they had administered him. His entire family gathered around him and had an intervention to make sure that his relapse could be controlled, and as a result, when he got better physically, they insisted that he go to the Betty Ford Clinic in Rancho Mirage, California, where he was admitted for his addiction. He was a patient there for 43 days.

I along with his manager Lou Robin and his wife Karen were probably the only non-family members permitted to go to the Betty Ford Clinic to visit Johnny Cash. I flew out to Palm Springs, rented a car and drove to the facility; it was a Sunday morning, and that was the only time when visitors were allowed. I felt privileged that Johnny thought that much of me to allow my visit in his time of crisis. He looked kind of rough, as he had just finished mopping the floor. As bad as he looked I could not believe how happy he was to see me. We sat down at a table and in a low voice so others could not hear him, he said, "Elizabeth Taylor is in here too, for some unknown reason." (I think she had a secret crush on him.) June had told me that every year on Johnny's birthday she would send him a card. In fact at his roast in Memphis in 1986, she purchased a gold page in the program and simply signed it Elizabeth.

Johnny completely recovered from both his medical problem as well as his addiction, at least for the time being. And to show his appreciation to the doctors and nurses, The Johnny Cash Show did a benefit concert in Palm Desert, California on April 24,1985. I know for I was there. Prior to the show, June went out of her way to introduce me to Colonel Tom Parker at the reception. Besides being Elvis's manager, he at one time had managed June Carter and also the Carter Family. They laughed as The Colonel reminded June of the time she played drums on Elvis's show. Folks, this is all part of country music's rich history that needs to preserved.

Chapter 7
Going Back to Church

From One Church to Another

This one's the story of how Johnny got me to go back to church. The story starts in Philadelphia, Mississippi in July of 1983, when I was an usher at the wedding of Johnny's long time guitar player and my friend Bob Wootton. Philadelphia is the town in Mississippi where three young civil rights leaders were murdered in June of 1954; as we northerners would say it's "a redneck town" full of pickup trucks with gun racks, and Confederate flag bumper stickers. Still, I loved it. It was my kind of place: very casual and laid back.

Anyway, to get to the wedding I first flew to Nashville and spent two days at Johnny's house before proceeding to a private airport in Gallatin, Tennessee. The weather was bad, and we had to await the arrival of a chartered Learjet to take all of us to Meridian, Mississippi. We entered the cabin of the private jet, and Johnny had a habit of looking at the photo and credentials, including hours flown, of both the pilot and copilot which were mounted on the wall just to our

left as we entered the aircraft. Johnny commented to me, "I like a pilot with a little gray in his hair, and a lot of hours in the air, makes me feel safer." Also traveling on the plane were John Carter, Marty Stuart, Marty's father and myself. Marty had been born in Philadelphia, so this was kind of like a homecoming for him and his dad.

The jet landed in Meridian where a van and chauffeur picked us up and made the hour long drive to Philadelphia. Upon arrival I proceed into a small room at the church to change into my tuxedo. (Several weeks before the wedding, I had faxed over to Bob the measurements, and it was awaiting my arrival).

Philadelphia is very hot and humid in July, and this day was no exception. But inside the church the air conditioning worked just fine. As the doors to the church opened and the wedding procession walked in, I saw to my amazement that there was a Confederate flag behind the altar, and the organist was not playing "Here Comes the Bride" but was playing "Dixie." Well, that was a real Southern wedding, and it went off without a hitch. During the ceremony Bob picked up a guitar and sang "Love Me Tender" to Vicky Cook, and soon they kissed as the preacher pronounced them man and wife.

After the wedding, there was a reception next door where I finally got to meet Vicky and soon realized why Bob had fallen in love with her. She was a beauty inside and out; very charming and friendly and she made you feel as if you'd known her your whole life. A hour or so later after partaking in some great Southern food and after cutting the wedding cake, the reception started to wind down. Johnny then turned to me and said, "Henry, you have to get back to New

Jersey don't you?" I replied, "yes" He said after we drop Marty and his father off at Gallatin, is it okay if we drop you off at Teterboro, as John Carter and I are going into the city for a few days?" This was 1983, and Johnny and June had an apartment in New York City on Central Park South, that they sublet from Liza Minnelli. In 1985 they gave it up and moved into the Berkeley Carteret Hotel, in Asbury Park.

Now the story gets interesting. After taking off from Gallatin we soared into the night. Flying on a Learjet is like being shot out of a cannon and riding a bullet, we soon reached a cruising altitude of 30,000 feet. I looked out the window and watched the world go by. Place yourself inside this ten-passenger plane, if you will. Up front the pilot and copilot flew the aircraft in front of a closed door. Directly behind them was the cabin with an aisle down the center, four plush seats on either side and a double couch-like seat at the very back. Johnny was sitting directly to my left in a single window seat; John Carter was curled up in the back, sleeping, and I was sitting opposite John looking out of the window. As I glanced over I saw that Johnny was reading the Bible. Now, I always tried to leave John alone, not wanting to be on top of him, just giving him some space and his privacy, as no matter where he went, people always seemed to want a piece of him.

About halfway through the flight, it starts to thunder and lightning and the plane is shaking. Johnny put down the Good Book he was reading and he turned to me and said, "Henry, I never hear you talk about God. What church do you go to?"

I was kind of startled by the question but I replied, Johnny, I don't go to church."

He said, "Why?"

I turned to him and kind of raised my right arm and made a downward motion with my hand and said ""It's a long story," I said. "You don't want to hear it."

Johnny said, "Yes I do."

Under my breath I said, *Oh shit, what am I going to tell this guy*? Of course, I told him the truth: I was brought up Catholic, went to Catholic grammar school, and got disenchanted with the church for several reasons. The main reason, I suppose, was that my company was building a large multimillion dollar Catholic Regional High School, St. Pius X, in a town called Piscataway,  N.J. There were some major design problems on the job and to cover them up, the architect tried to throw me off the job. The job was stopped for several weeks before I had an audience with the Bishop, who was the head of the Diocese of Trenton at the Chancery office in Lawrenceville, N.J. His name was George W. Ahr, Bishop of Trenton, and at the meeting I knelt down kissed his ring, and did all the right stuff.

During the meeting the Bishop said, "Young man", I was about twenty eight at the time "I need my school finished immediately. How can we work this out to get you back on the job and get the school completed?" After meeting about an hour or so with a third party engineer present, it was agreed that the architect would make some corrective drawings, and the new engineer would approve them and take them to the building department to reinstate the permit. I will never forget the Bishop's confident words: "I want you to go back to work; we will pay you and work out all our differences and problems at the end of the job, as I need to get my school opened." After the corrective drawings were made and the permit was reinstated we went back to work and finished the job. But guess what: they never paid me.

I told Johnny that I'd sued; the church in superior court and I emphasized that I won, as I was *proud* to have taken on an entity as powerful as the Church and beat them. Johnny's comment (I will never forget his words, either): "Henry, remember something: the Bishop is only a mortal man, and he sins too. But there is a God up there, and you should go back to church."

I said, "You're right." I probably yessed him to death, praying to both God and the Bishop and whoever else that he would change the subject, which he finally did. Johnny's remarks, truthfully, at that time about me going to church went in one ear and out the other. It is important to remember that this time period was referred to as the "Go-Go Eighties." I was a major contractor and developer, and everything I touched turned to gold (the problem I found out later, is that it was only Fool's Gold). I was a big shot back then: I owned a house on the ocean in Deal N.J., a guitar factory, an industrial park, a major construction company, a hotel, several office buildings, and was a partner in a billion dollar-redevelopment project in my hometown of Asbury Park. In plain English, I was on top of the world and thought my shit didn't stink.

Cover Story in New Jersey Monthly Magazine 1985

Thus, I didn't need church, or anybody to lecture me about church, not even Johnny Cash. The flight continued without further incident, an hour or so later the pilot lowered the wheels and flaps and our Learjet landed safely at Teterboro airport.

Johnny and John Carter went to New York City and I returned home to Asbury Park. Things continued to flourish for me during the rest of the eighties. Johnny and June spent a lot of time in Asbury Park. Our families went on several vacations and fishing trips together in the Bahamas. And I would spend much of my free time, as June would say, "paddling around" with them on their tour bus. And life was good. However, all good things must come to an end.

To jump ahead with my own story a little bit. By the late '80's my little world started to come apart big time. I was having problems with Carabetta Enterprises, my partner in the billion dollar Asbury Park Beachfront Redevelopment project. The success of the Berkeley Carteret Hotel was directly tied to the beachfront redevelopment, as it sat 200 feet from the convention hall that was scheduled to be renovated. Back then the convention hall hosted many trade shows which directly and indirectly fed business to the hotel, either in the form of rooms or food and beverage. These renovations never happened. In fact, for several years the hall was closed down and all the trade shows left, leaving the hotel standing alone, as if on its own island. In a quick series of events, without that added income the hotel eventually filed for bankruptcy. Under the bankruptcy code Chapter 11 allowed us as debtor in possession to continue to operate the hotel until it was finally converted to a Chapter 7 and sold at a sheriff sale.

Singer Johnny Cash My Friend John Stood By My Side Asbury Park Press/Sun., April 17, 1963 E3

'As long as Henry Vaccaro is involved, so will I be'

Q. How involved are you in A.P. Boardwalk Associates' (contractor Henry V. Vaccaro's group) efforts to purchase Asbury Park's oceanfront properties? Can you tell us what your investment is — or will be?

CASH: My involvement in Asbury Park's redevelopment came about through my friendship with Henry Vaccaro. My investment is mainly the time I will devote to it.

" Q. And what role do you expect to play in the acquisition and restoration of the 57-year-old Berkeley Carteret Hotel?

CASH: My wife, June Carter, and our son, John Carter, will have a permanent apartment in the hotel for vacations or for when we have business or concerts in the Northeast United States.

Q. The Asbury Park City Council has decided to appeal the court's ruling barring the city from selling its boardwalk area property to A.P. Boardwalk Associates. If the case gets tied up in litigation for a long period of time, is there a possibility you will lose your interest and bow out?

CASH: No, never. As long as Henry Vaccaro is involved, so will I be.

Q. What motivated you to join the

Press Conference

JOHNNY CASH, singer who is a member of a group seeking to buy municipally-owned property adjacent to the Asbury Park boardwalk, is today's Press Conference subject.

Each week a different celebrity or person in the news is featured, and readers are invited to participate by submitting questions.

Next Sunday's subject will be Dina Merrill, co-star of the hit Broadway show "On Your Toes," and on May 1, singer Lorna Luft, star of the off-Broadway show "Snoopy" and daughter of the late Judy Garland and theatrical agent Sid Luft.

Questions should be mailed to Press Conference, Asbury Park Sunday Press, Press Plaza, Asbury Park, N.J. 07712.

Q. Who gave you your first opportunity to perform?

CASH: Elvis Presley in Memphis in 1955.

Q. How do you and your wife, manage to balance your private and professional lives? How will the contract you recently signed to do an album with your wife affect your lives?

CASH: We leave the business at the office when we are home.

Q. Your son, John Carter, is 13 now. Has he ever discussed the possibility of becoming an entertainer? If so, what was your reaction?

Q. What are your future recording plans?

CASH: I just finished recording an album in Los Angeles produced by Brian Ahern, Emmy Lou Harris' husband and a well-known record producer. I plan to record as long as God gives me a voice.

CASH: He sings on all the summer shows. He seems to have a natural knack for it but as you said, he's 13, so I will let him decide for himself later.

Q. What is the greatest inconvenience you face as a performer and/or celebrity?

CASH: Finding time to be alone to be able to think, write, meditate and pray more often and to know the right moves to make and the right words to say.

Army reviews new rifle training

The Associated Press

COLUMBUS, Ga. — After spending $4.5 million to develop more sophisticated pop-up targets to train infantry riflemen, the Army now is considering a plan to incorporate the old bull's-eye target into the new system.

The new Infantry Remoted Target System is designed to simulate battlefield conditions by surprising a rifle trainee with electronically controlled targets that pop

hit-or-miss information, not the precise bullet locations feedback that is necessary for the development of good marksmanship skills," rifle expert Art Osborne wrote in "Infantry" magazine last year.

Because of the problem posed by the lack of such feedback, the Army Research Institute at Fort Benning near here, is considering testing a bull's-eye target as a companion or substitute for parts of the new system.

few shots to see exactly where the bullets hit.

But that proved to be a time-consuming exercise, one that was described by Osborne as a "poor boy" solution to the feedback problem.

Dr. Seward Smith, director of the Army Research Institute at Fort Benning, helped invent the pop-up target in the 1950s while assigned to the Institute's forerunner, the Human Resources Research Office.

Smith said pop-up targets first were de-

Due to financial pressure I was forced to sell out my partnership interest in the redevelopment project to Carabetta for nine million dollars in secured notes; one million a year for nine years. I thought that I was set for life.

Surprise, surprise. My partner Carabetta then went bankrupt and all the notes were worthless. I tried to hang on for a year or so but couldn't, my choices were pretty slim, so on November 8, 1991 I filed for personal bankruptcy protection in a Chapter 11 proceeding and attempted to reorganize and salvage whatever I could. Things did not work out as several banks that I dealt with also failed and were taken over by the FDIC. They would not cooperate in helping me restructure as all the FDIC wanted was to sell off my real estate at any price to get quick cash.

HOUSE OF CASH

POST OFFICE BOX 508 • HENDERSONVILLE, TENNESSEE 37077 • PHONE (615) 824-5110

To Whom It May Concern
% Henry V. Vaccaro
3320 Highway 66
Neptune, NJ 07753

January 9, 1990

I have been involved with Henry Vaccaro both as his friend and partner since the inception of the Berkley-Carteret Hotel. In fact, June and I have performed concerts in the Convention Hall to bring awareness to the redevelopment of Asbury Park as well as to the Berkley-Carteret Hotel. We maintain an apartment at the Hotel and spend as much time there as our travels permit and we love it!

This letter will serve as our firm commitment to help Henry Vaccaro in any way possible to achieve his goal of creating Asbury Park as the music center of the East.

Henry and I have talked at great length of planning a spa and recording facilities adjacent to the Hotel and I am behind him in all of his endeavors.

Kindest regards.

Very truly yours,

Johnny Cash

Johnny Cash

JC/rh

John Demonstrating his Continued Support for Me and My Dreams For Asbury Park

In 1996 my personal chapter 11 was converted to what is called a Chapter 7 which means everything you own is liquidated and sold off. When they got finished with me I lost my construction company, industrial park and all my real estate holdings. As if that was not bad enough, my partner in the guitar company embezzled a lot of money and left me with the debt as I had personally guaranteed a bank loan of 3.5 million. I had no options left but to put my last remaining asset, Kramer Guitar Company, whose ownership was in a corporate name into bankruptcy. When that happened I was broke, not only broke-broke, but also flat-broke, out-and-out broke, and every other kind of broke.

Now for the punch line, one Sunday morning, back in 1989 before the bankruptcy's I woke up around 8 a.m. As I lay in bed I heard Johnny's voice in my head: "Henry, go to church." so I put on the TV, turned over, pulled up the covers and went back to sleep. About 11 a.m., I again awoke and heard his voice again "Henry, go to church." I had chills this time, and didn't know what to make of it but I quickly dressed, and drove the mile or so to Our Lady of Mount Carmel Church in Asbury Park, one of the hardest thing I ever did. I snuck in the side door so no one would see me; that's how ashamed I felt. When I got into church I sat in the last pew, and all of a sudden it was as if God's hand had touched me. A calming, peaceful feeling came over me, my worries seemed to disappear, and through the grace of God I was able to cope with my tremendous financial pressure. That was in 1989 and I have not missed church since.

Sometime afterward, out of the clear blue sky, June called me to let me know that she, Johnny, and John Carter were coming to the hotel for a week, and asked if I could arrange for a limo to pick them up at Newark Airport that Friday. I told June that I would personally pick them up and to please tell Johnny that I'd gone back to church. In her Southern drawl, June said "He will be so proud of you!"

I thought nothing of her comment, but I arrived at Newark airport in my car, and soon John sat in the front seat, June and John Carter in the rear. We had just pulled out of the airport when John turned to me and said, "June said you went back to church?" I replied that I did, and John asked if it was tough. I told him it had been very awkward. John then asked "what service do you go too" I replied the 10:30 Mass. John then said "Come by the hotel on Sunday and pick me up; I'm going with you."

Well you guessed it on Sunday morning Johnny Cash who is Southern Baptist, along with John Carter, went with me to Our Lady of Mount Carmel, a Catholic church. Johnny attended church with me the last five times he ever came to Asbury Park, N.J. including the Sunday morning in 1992 after he'd been inducted into the Rock and Roll Hall of Fame the preceding Saturday night, at the Waldorf Astoria Hotel in New York City.

Father Dan at Billy Graham's Crusade in Central Park NYC

When I first went back to church, I was very inspired by a new priest, Father Daniel Houde. When he gave a sermon, you listened. I befriended Father Daniel and as we had dinner one night, Daniel turned to me and said, "I know Johnny Cash is your idol."

"Yes he is, Father. Who is your idol?"

His response, which shocked me, was "Billy Graham is my idol." I said that's surprising, Daniel said I would love to meet him someday."

Here we go again, Johnny invited me to attend Billy Graham's Crusade on Sept. 22, 1991 in Central Park. I asked Johnny if he had room for Father Dan, and he said. "Of course, bring him along." After the 10:30 Mass I picked up Daniel and it was off to New York, to the Plaza Athenee Hotel, where the Cash's were staying. June had a light lunch sent up in the room for us. After lunch, we hopped into John's limo, and with all five of us in the car, headed to Central Park through a private entrance toward the backstage area. John's driver, Curt pulled up alongside a trailer. Which was used as a dressing room for John and June, and it was adjacent to, and in front of Billy Graham's trailer.

Johnny invited Father Dan and me inside and lo and behold, who comes walking by but Billy Graham on the way to his trailer. John and Billy spotted each other and they embraced like two lost brothers. June joined them, and after some small talk, Johnny said, "I want you to meet a good friend of mine, Father Daniel from Asbury Park, New Jersey." A few seconds later Father Daniel was introduced to his idol, Billy Graham, thanks to my idol, Johnny Cash. That night after the crusade, we all had dinner together, and the rest is history.

A very Happy Father Dan with Johnny

One other thing while at Johnny's home in June of 1995 we were just sitting around at the counter in his kitchen and the subject of my bankruptcy came up Johnny looked at me and said Henry remember something *"The only thing that went bankrupt was your wallet"* He then pointed to my heart and then my forehead *"as long as that heart of yours continues to pump and as long as that brain of yours keeps working you will come back bigger and stronger than before"* Thanks to John who reintroduced me to my faith and the power of prayer which allowed me to survive the Great Roller Coaster Ride of Life, and turned me into a survivor.

51

Chapter 8
Square-Headed Grouper
Folks, This Ain't No Fish Story

This story takes place in my favorite Bahamian Out Island of Bimini, which is the closest foreign soil to mainland Florida. I became aware of this island paradise in 1960, when I made my first trip to this world-renowned fishing spot, it has been reported that more world's record fish have been caught in Bimini than any other place in the world. But over the years, Bimini began to change, and in many ways not for the better. In those early years you could walk the King's Highway *(not really a highway but a narrow street maybe 14 feet wide)* where all the natives would greet you with a smile and a "Good day, sir." You could leave your door unlocked as there was very little crime on this island.

Bimini is separated into two islands, north and south. North Bimini is where the natives live; it is broken down into several small areas, namely Bailey Town, Alice Town, Porgy Bay and Paradise Point. Mostly all the hotels and marinas are located there. South Bimini contains a few residential homes and the airport, if you want to call it that. There is no electricity, water or

Air View of North Bimini

sewer; individual generators provide power on South Bimini. In the '70s, because of its location, Bimini became a haven for illegal drugs from Colombia and their trafficking to the US mainland. I will give you several examples Many times I would see the customs agent, a native whose salary was about $25,000 a year, with more gold around his neck than Mr. T, wearing a Rolex Presidential watch with real diamonds—you can only imagine what went down.

Now bear in mind this is a poor island, whose inhabitants earn their living from the ocean or the tourist trade. The island is only maybe five miles long and a half mile at its widest, with only two roads: the King's Highway, all 14 feet in width running along the southern side of the island, and the Queen's Highway, about 12 feet wide on the northern side. The chief immigration officer, also a native, owned a Mercedes convertible with a TV in it, had the same amount of gold as the customs guy, and lived in a two-story home on the water's edge. He could only drive the

Johnny Saying Hello to One of the Locals

car from his house to the seaplane ramp and back, a total of about two miles. In the marina it was not uncommon to find several fast speedboats called "cigarette hulls." These were custom-built boats with large covered decks and three high-speed engines designed to carry drugs and outrace the Coast Guard. They could cost upwards of five hundred thousand dollars each. They were the modern version of the old rumrunner, also called a "go-fast boat."

53

A Go-Fast Boat Being Chased by the Coast Guard

Now pan across the bay to South Bimini and the airport. On any given day you could find several planes that had either crashed there at night because there were no runway lights or had been seized by the government and pushed aside off the single runway by a front-end loader and piled up. The local shops on Bimini sold T-shirts with the slogan "Save the Bales." as opposed to "Save the Whales" printed on them.

One beautiful sunny day in Bimini, there was hardly any breeze with calm seas. It was a perfect day to go after "the Big Ones." And on this particular trip my guests were Johnny Cash, John Carter Cash, Bob Wootton and Gene Nieto. We all were staying at the Bimini Big Game Fishing Club, where I was a member. All of us had just eaten breakfast at the club and Johnny said, "Why don't you guys go on without me, as I would like to lie around the pool, just relax and do some writing." John Carter also decided to stay with his dad, so the rest of us were off to the yacht *Falcon*, a short five-minute walk to Weech's dock where the boat is berthed.

After bidding good morning to Mr. Jerry, the dock master, we jumped on the *Falcon* and were greeted by Captain Jimmy and Willie Pinder, our mate, and a very good mate he was. In preparation for our fishing trips, Willie would make up fresh baits just for us.

My common practice on these trips was to arrive early in the afternoon on the first day. The plan was to take Chalk's seaplane from Government Cut in Miami for the half-hour flight to Bimini Bay, where we would land on the water before taxiing up the ramp on North Bimini. This would allow at least a few hours in the afternoon to fish around the reefs for fresh bait with light-spinning tackle. It was not uncommon to catch mackerel, yellowtail and bonefish there in the two- to three-pound range, which was perfect for marlin bait.

Johnny seeing us off

Captain Jimmy had trained Willie Pinder over the years in the art of making baits. This was a real art, and I enjoyed watching the show. Willie would first slice the underside of the fresh caught fish, gut it, and place two very large hooks linked together in the cavity, then push a wire through the mouth and attach it to the top hook. After pulling this leader wire tight, he would proceed to sew up the fish with a large needle attached to a foot of dental floss. I swear, you would think Willie was a surgeon. His next step was to break the backbone of the baitfish and wiggle it, so when it was in the water it would seem to swim and move like a live fish. The last thing he did was to pop out the eyes. Willie would make up about 10 or 12 fresh baits each morning and put them on ice for us as we needed them.

Me Showing Off the Freshly Sutured Baits

Now with the prep work done and the *Falcon* all fueled up, off to the fishing grounds we went. The *Falcon* was a 50-foot all-wood twin diesel-powered vessel, with a large cockpit from which to fish. The cockpit contained an open area about 12 feet wide and 14 feet long from the transom (the rear section of the hull connecting both sides) to the cabin area. It had a massive fighting chair with an adjustable footrest that was bolted to the center deck, about four feet from the rear transom. There were also two swiveling lighter duty fishing chairs mounted to the rear of the fighting chair, one on each side just in front of the cabin. The main cabin was wide open to the rear while sliding glass enclosed the sides and the front had a fixed windshield. It contained two very comfortable custom mattresses lying directly on top of the motor compartments.

All the controls for operating the vessel were topside on the flying bridge. Three steps down were the head (toilet, for you non-seamen) and two smaller bunks. Top side, covering the entire cabin, was a flying bridge with the wheel and throttle, where Captain Jimmy would operate the boat. This height also allowed him greater visibility to spot fish in the water with his trained eyes. The bridge was accessible only by a fixed ladder on the right side of the deck. On top of the flying bridge was a canvas top mounted on an aluminum frame to shade you from the hot Caribbean sun. This type of canvas covering is known all over the world as a "Bimini Top".

The *Falcon* was a great boat to fish from, as it had two thirty foot outriggers, one mounted on each side of the cabin which, when extended, permitted four additional baits in the water, spread far enough apart as not to get tangled with each other. In theory we could fish five lines at the same time, some with different size baits like the smaller ballyhoo. Ballyhoo is frozen bait used for fish like sailfish, wahoo, etc., but it has been my experience that the fresh bait attracts more fish.

What's nice about fishing off Bimini are the crystal clear water, the many reefs and the closeness of the Gulf Stream to the island, which permits you to start fishing literally 15 to 20 minutes from the dock. Well, on that day, after dragging our baits in the water for over an hour or so we only got one strike: Bob Wootton brought in a 20-pound barracuda, we fished the rest of the morning with no other strikes. Soon Captain Jimmy came up with a new strategy: we would go over an old wreck that he knew of and try fishing for grouper with a wire line. Grouper live and swim among the wrecks and around rocks where they can hide; that's why a wire line is used, so it can't get cut in the deep water, near the bottom. This was a smart decision, as we caught several nice-sized grouper and a 40-pound amberjack.

The Falcon docked at Weech's

Several hours later, Captain Jimmy is on the move again, this time to a weed line he'd spotted a mile or so offshore. He saw some birds working, and usually where there are birds, there are fish. Small fish sometimes feed off these weed lines and as expected, bigger fish like dolphin (*Mahi Mahi*) feed off the smaller fish. A weed line is usually formed when weeds, sea grass and floating debris collect where two dissimilar ocean currents meet each other, forcing the weeds together and then they all flow north with the faster and more powerful gulfstream, much like a riptide.

I was down in the cockpit, strapped into the fighting chair, harness and fishing pole in hand with fresh mackerel as bait on the line, and two long outriggers on each side of the boat dragging smaller baits. These were connected to the fishing poles that Bob Wootton and Gene Nieto were holding as they sat anxious in the smaller fishing chairs behind me. Captain Jimmy, up on the flying bridge, pulled alongside the weed line looking for signs of fish when all of a sudden he yelled, "Willie get the flying gaff!" (A flying gaff is an 8-foot aluminum pole with a giant hook on the end, attached to a three quarter-inch rope. Once the hook is engaged in a fish, the aluminum handle will disengage leaving the hook and rope attached to the quarry.) "I see some square-headed grouper floating in the weed line!" Captain Jimmy yelled as the boat slowed down. Willie held the handle as he put the flying gaff in the water and lo and behold, pulled on board a 50-pound bale of marijuana all wrapped in several waterproof layers of plastic so it would float. Jimmy yelled "I see some more!" and we pulled alongside another, another, and another until we had on board a total of seven bales of marijuana.

First Mate Willie Pinder

Evidently, a drug plane had flown over at night and dropped the bales into the sea, expecting a cigarette boat to retrieve them (which did not happen, for some unknown reason). Each one of these bales was not only waterproof and could float but were equipped with some sort of electronic homing device to make it easier for the drug boat to locate them. "Damn!" Captain Jimmy said, "This is better than fishing." With seven square-headed grouper on board the *Falcon,* the Captain told Willie to cover the bales with a tarp as we headed back to Bimini.

Now here's the problem: we have a boatload of marijuana, and Johnny Cash and John Carter waiting back at the dock to see our catch of actual fish. What the hell do we do? Well, Captain Jimmy pulled along side the end of Weech's dock, not at his regular berth, and quickly let Bob, Gene and myself off like nothing ever happened. I told Johnny that we caught several fish, nothing over 40 pounds, and that Captain Jimmy had to go to another dock to fuel up, and would join us later. I didn't let him know what really happened until we got back to the Big Game Club and were having dinner, as I felt that would give me enough time to think up a cover story. But I soon decided that I should be honest and tell the truth.

At first Johnny was a little pissed, and said how could I do that with all of us traveling and fishing together? But then he thought about it a while later and started laughing. "Hell, when I was younger I did worse than that, but I got caught!" (Back in 1965, Johnny was arrested for bringing his guitar case full of amphetamines from Mexico into the States.)

Captain Jimmy, now with a boatload of marijuana, took off toward the backwaters of Bimini, out of sight from everyone, where the stuff was sold for $3,000 per bale. To quote Captain Jimmy, "We had a very profitable trip."

So, my friends, if you're ever asked in a trivia quiz what a "square-headed grouper" is, you will probably be the only one with the correct answer. Since this episode happened over 25 years ago, the statute of limitations has now expired, and that's why I can so freely tell this story. This has to be true as no one could make this crap up.

Part of The Days Catch, A Taped up Bale of "Square Headed Grouper" under the tarp

Chapter 9
We Buy for Cash
We Sell for Cash

The year was 1985, and things were still in pretty bad shape in Asbury Park. Not too much was going on, but at least now everyone had hope, because recently there was so much positive press with the announcement that the massive beachfront redevelopment contract was signed, the restoration of the Berkeley Carteret Hotel was in full swing, and Johnny Cash had taken to visiting the city.

A featured story appeared in *New Jersey Monthly* magazine called "W e l c o m e t o V a c c a r o l a n d" which talked about Johnny Cash and TV anchorman Ernie Anastos and their support and investment in the Berkeley. There was a man named Tony Houston who had only recently moved to town, and he opened an antique store in a vacant building located on the southwest corner of Main Street and Sewell Avenue, just down the street from the firehouse. At one time, this building housed a company called Checker Stores, which sold automotive accessories, bicycles and small household appliances.

When Tony first opened for business, he had signs in the window that read "Merchandise and Antiques for sale: We buy for cash, we sell for cash." So now, after all the publicity surrounding Johnny Cash at the city council meeting and his commitment to not only invest but to live part time in the Berkeley (at that point, Johnny and June lived in Tennessee most of the time but also had a winter home in Jamaica), Tony thought it would be appropriate to put up a giant sign that filled both windows and said: "We Need Johnny Cash and We Need Him Now"

The Grand Ballroom at the Berkeley Carteret Hotel

Well one afternoon Johnny and June decided to come to Asbury Park to check out the renovations underway in the hotel. They drove down from their apartment in New York City in a limousine, anxious to see the progress being made with their new east coast home in Asbury Park. It was late afternoon when they arrived and they spent a couple hours walking through the building.

John marveled at the progress that had been made since his last visit: the ballrooms on the second level, consisting of the magnificent 500 seat Crystal Ballroom and adjoining Continental and Bradley Ballrooms were almost completed; the new plaster moldings had been installed; the ceilings were painted; the custom designed Axminster carpet had arrived from London and was rolled up in the corner covered by a tarp. Three new crystal chandeliers from Czechoslovakia were still in their protective crates, awaiting installation.

The big plus was that the elevators were now working and could take Johnny and June to their new eighth floor home. June opened the door which had two gold stars on it, his and hers, and as she entered, a reporter from the *Asbury Park Press* followed her into the apartment so she could do an interview.

I'll try to describe the layout of the Cash apartment. As you entered there was a foyer in the center, and off to the right was a full-sized kitchen. To the left was a large master bedroom with a full bath, including a Jacuzzi tub. As you walked straight ahead, you'd enter this massive 20 by 50 combination living area and open dining room that spanned the entire width of the southeast wing of the hotel. Also off the foyer,

June and I Touring The Cash's Soon to Be Penthouse

just before the kitchen, was a locked common door that gave access to a standard hotel room that they could use if needed for a guest, it was locked and rented for hotel use when they were not in residence.

June could not believe the size of the apartment, let alone the beautiful view of the ocean that it had. The *Press* reporter was interested in June's thoughts of Asbury Park, how much time they planned on spending at the hotel, and how she planned on decorating the apartment. One of June's main objectives that day, besides seeing the hotel, was to pick out the color of their carpet.

Photos Courtesy of Dave Gamble

She called me a week before their visit to get different samples, all of them blue. June claimed to like a color called "Hot Blue," but she eventually picked out a sample called Dresden Blue, which we then ordered and had installed.

PANORAMA

Johnny Cash, 'home' in Asbury Park

By JILL HAND
Press Staff Writer

The elegant Berkeley-Carteret Hotel on the oceanfront in Asbury Park is an unlikely place to find a pair of down-home country musicians. But when Johnny Cash and his wife, June Carter Cash, are in the Northeast, "home" lies behind two big brass stars on the door to their eighth-floor suite here.

The stars on the door are a bit of show business whimsy that sprang from the fertile imagination of Cash's friend, Henry V. Vaccaro, the moving force behind Asbury Park's redevelopment. Vaccaro is the principal of A.P. Boardwalk Associates Inc., the corporation that bought the 60-year-old red brick hotel for $325,000 in 1983 and spent more than two years and $14 million transforming it from an eyesore into a showplace.

Other doors in the 259-room hotel bear a single star, marking them as corporate suites, but the Cashes' door is unique in having two, identifying it as the domain of a duo who get top billing wherever they go.

"At first, they were going to have one star, but I thought June should have one, too," Vaccaro said

JOHNNY CASH

LET'S VISIT

After the visit, it was time to leave the hotel and head over to Christie's restaurant in the next town of Wanamassa for dinner. Christopher Meccia, a very close friend of mine, owned the restaurant and arranged to seat all of us in a private dining area. Since both Johnny and June loved Italian food. Christie's was the perfect choice, and Chris, as he liked to be called, was himself a gourmet chef.

I joined Johnny and June along with my daughter Toni in the limousine for the short ten-minute drive. On the way to Wanamassa, we drove down Main Street in Asbury Park and passed directly in front of Tony Houston's antique store, where I then pointed out the sign in the window. June screamed, "Stop the car!"

Johnny With My Dear Friend Christie

"Why John, we have to go in that store," so Curt the driver nervously pulled the car over and parked, and we all got out. Thank God I always had a camera with me; I got a priceless picture of Johnny next to the sign reading *We Need Johnny Cash Now.*

I guess it was around 6 o'clock in the evening and the store was closed. Johnny walked over to the front door and knocked, and we all heard this voice from inside saying, "I'm sorry, but we're *closed*."

Johnny knocked again, and we heard "Hey buddy, I don't think you understand English. We are *closed*." Not one to be discouraged, Johnny knocked a third time and the voice got angrier: "You don't fucking understand English, buddy: We are *closed*!" Johnny leaned down to the open keyhole, cupped his hands to his mouth, and in that deep Johnny Cash voice said, "Excuse me sir, I see by the sign in the window you're looking for me, *WELL, HERE I AM.*"

Now this guy, Tony Houston, opened the door and let out a scream that you could have heard in Nashville. He yelled, "Oh my God, it's Johnny Cash!" The guy's wife came running down the open staircase from the second floor, so excited that she's got her right shoe on her left foot, and tripped coming down. It was incredible; just like a scene out of *Amos and Andy* or *I love Lucy.*

Johnny After Surprising the Store Owners

63

Tony Houston and his wife over time became good friends with John and June because they dealt in collectibles and June herself was an avid antique dealer back home in Hendersonville, Tennessee. June had purchased a turn-of-the-century old railroad station that had been scheduled for demolition and had it moved to the House of Cash where she set it

up as an antique shop. Besides being a great entertainer, June was a brilliant businessperson, buying and selling antiques that she had collected from all over the world. Their home in Hendersonville on Old Hickory Lake was packed full of world-class antiques. I spent the night there on several occasions and slept in

"The Lincoln Bed." I always thought that the Lincoln Bed was in the White House, but I soon found out from June that there were *three* Lincoln Beds: one was in the White House and Johnny Cash owned the other two. Well, so much for history. This story demonstrated some of the exciting things that happened "When Johnny Cash came to Town."

Me in Johnny and June's Guest Bedroom

Chapter 10

My Surprise 45th Birthday Party

Boy, time sure goes by fast when you're having fun. Here I am now 72 years old, thinking and writing about my 45th surprise birthday party held on Monday, September 2, 1985. Not only was this a surprise, but a shock. I was divorced at the time and had spent the day with my son Henry Jr. at the beach in Asbury Park, across the street from the Berkeley Carteret Hotel.

Around mid-afternoon, Henry began nagging me to take him to his mother's house in neighboring Ocean Township. It was such a nice beach day, the last day of the summer season, and I wasn't in any hurry.

I had recently found and restored a 1958 red and white Corvette, just like the one I'd had when I was 16 years old, and I had taken her out that day. So I took my time enjoying the ride and decided on the way home I would stop at a friend's, Asbury Park Mayor Frank Fiorentino, just to shoot the breeze. But when I got there, he rushed me out of his house, saying he and Josie his wife had to leave. A little dejected, I decided to just take Henry Jr. back to

Me in The '58 Vette

his mom's. I drove the five minutes to Diane's house, still dressed in beach attire, turned the corner to her house, saw a lot of cars there, and thought nothing of it until I opened the yard gate to the swimming pool and was totally shocked to find all my friends yelling *"Surprise!"*

This was the surprise of a lifetime. Besides all my immediate family and friends, including some I had not seen for years, there was the entire executive staff from the Berkeley Carteret Hotel which had just opened. And one of the biggest surprises was to see my friend Ernie Anastos and his wife Kelly. Ernie was the anchorman on the WABC-TV Channel 7 News out of New York. His wife Kelly was from Asbury Park, and her father was the pastor of the Greek Orthodox Church there. They had met when Ernie was in the army and stationed at Fort Monmouth.

All of a sudden I heard the familiar sound of my favorite local band, the Squan River Band, and as I turned to get a better view, who do you think I spotted sitting down at the table near the band with my mother: none other than June Carter Cash. I had just said goodbye to John and June the day before as they were heading back to Nashville, or so I thought, not realizing June was staying behind purposely to attend my surprise party. This whole thing was a fantastic surprise.

There are not many men I know whose ex-wife would throw them a party, never mind one of this magnitude. I felt truly blessed. The food was fantastic, as the hotel's executive chef, Miklos Kiss, had prepared it, and the birthday cake came from the pastry chef. The music of course was great, as the Squan River Band, my favorite country band, outside of the Tennessee Three. d I used to see them perform at a little country joint called Kiefer's Country Inn on Squankum Road in Howell, New Jersey.

June and I at the Party

My friend Shad Woolley headed the band, which came in 2nd out of 2,100 bands in a national Wild Turkey Shooters contest held in Nashville. The next thing I knew, Shad hit the chord to "Wabash Cannonball," and June got up from the table, took over the microphone and sang the original Carter Family version of this classic country song. Need I say more? There will never be another birthday party like that one.

Thank you Diane, and thank you June Carter Cash, wherever you are.

JOHNNY CASH *Sept / 1985*

Dear Henry

Happy Birthday

Sorry I couldnt be there.

Here is the first copy of my new Album, "Rainbow" which will be released next month.

Have a great day,

your Friend,

Johny Cash

Chapter 11
The Day the Johnny Cash Show Came to Town

Photo by Robert Siliato

Back in 1983 when we first discussed an investment in the Berkeley Carteret Hotel, Johnny said, "When you get that hotel up and running, when you get control of that convention center, and the Paramount Theater, I want to open it for you." Well, as I told him, I would not let Johnny perform a concert for nothing, so we entered into a written contract with one of our holding companies, Host Realty Co., and paid him the going rate for his show. In turn, Johnny and June made an investment in the hotel, many, many times larger than the fee that was charged for the concert.

True to his word, on October 18, 1985 The Johnny Cash Show rolled into Asbury Park and set up shop at the Paramount Theater on the boardwalk for two sold-out shows, timed to coincide with the grand opening of the Berkeley. As previously mentioned, the hotel sat caddy-corner directly across the street from this classic theater, which formed a part of a larger convention center. The Asbury Park Convention Hall, the Paramount Theater, and the Berkeley Carteret Hotel were all conceived and built to complement each other by the famed New York architects Warren and Wetmore, who made their mark as the designers of the Grand Central Station in New York City.

I was standing outside the Paramount when a huge black and silver Peterbilt tractor, attached to a sleek all-black trailer, pulled up to the stage door on the Ocean Avenue side of the building. The trailer had elegantly painted lettering in silver: "The Johnny Cash Show" on both

Wirehead

sides. A closer look at the tractor revealed a small decal, indicating that it was powered by a Caterpillar diesel engine, and the driver's handle, "Wirehead," was also painted in small maroon letters under the driver's side window. To see this truck with that "Johnny Cash Show" name in my hometown was a sight to behold, something I waited my whole life to see.

I knew all the guys that worked as roadies for John, as they also doubled as sound and light engineers and guitar technicians during the show. The crew, led by Jay Dauro from Huntsville, Alabama, along with Kent Elliott, Larry Johnson and Brian Farmer, had all

The Johnny Cash Show Head Roadie Jay Dauro

been with the show as long as I can remember. They all had one thing in common: they loved their job and they loved working for Johnny Cash.

I always enjoyed watching them unload all the gear and set up the stage; they'd done it so many times all over the world and could probably do it blindfolded. John's trailer carried everything required for a show anywhere, from an outdoor stage on a large field to a stadium or a theater. This truck had sound equipment, lighting, stage props, a movie projector, generator, all types of musical instruments, guitars (both electric and acoustic), fiddle, horns, autoharp and even a grand piano. It also carried

all the T-shirts, records, programs and souvenirs that were sold at the shows. After the truck was unloaded, the crew could usually set up the show in about four hours.

It was about 6 o'clock, an hour before show time, when John walked into the Paramount with June. The first thing they did before going to their dressing room was step onto the stage. Johnny marveled at this beautiful old theater. Even though he'd been in it in 1983, he'd forgotten how beautiful the theater was and how amazing

Inside the Beautiful Paramount Theater

69

the acoustics were. Jay, his chief sound guy, went up in the balcony and said he could hear Johnny on stage talking to June, and there was no amplification at all. They both then retired to their dressing rooms to get ready. One by one, the guys in the band walked over from the hotel: Bob Wootton, Marty Stuart, Earl Poole Ball, Jimmy Tittle, W.S. Holland, Jack Hale Jr. and Bob Lewin. They walked through the stage door and started to check things out on stage before the show.

On the other side of the curtain, the audience was filling into their seats for the first of two sold-out shows. Many students from Asbury Park High School had volunteered as ushers. It's almost show time as the lights dim on and off as a signal for everyone to take their seats. With the lights off and the theater almost completely dark, the curtain slowly rose as Earl Poole Ball on the piano kicked off this medley of Johnny Cash hits, and the stage lights slowly came on as one by one the band joined in. First, with Bob Wootton on his Kramer guitar, then Marty Stuart and Jimmy Tittle on bass accompanied by the "Father of the Drums," W.S. Holland, and finally the horns of Jack Hale and Bob Lewin.

As soon as they finished, with the place now completely quiet, a tall dark figure emerged with his back to the crowd, a guitar slung over his shoulder. As the spotlight shone on center stage, the figure turned around and in that thundering voice said, "Hello, I'm Johnny Cash." The audience exploded with applause as he started singing "Ring of Fire."

Johnny performed at two sold-out shows that night and they were both spectacular. We hired a local TV station to film the perform- ances, and I con- verted my copies to DVD. There are several sig- nificant things I remember about these shows. My friend Ernie An- astos, the an-

chorman on the ABC news from New York, took time off from his news broadcast to come to Asbury Park and act as the Master of Ceremonies for the event. Ernie's wife Kelly grew up in Asbury, so he adopted it as his second hometown.

Also Mayor Frank Fiorentino was there; he gave Johnny the key to the City of Asbury Park. The Mayor was a special guy, for Asbury Park which is a close-knit community and a spe- cial guy to my family and me. I had known Frank all my life. When I was a kid, he was a patient and friend of my father's and he'd set up my Lionel train set. Frank was also the plant manager at a large concrete block manufacturer from where I purchased over a million dollars in block when I was in the construction business. Frank has always been like an uncle to me.

But the most memorable moment was during the show when Johnny took a break and June came on stage. June just captivated the audience, had them eating out of her hand. June came on, took the microphone and started talking about how she met me, about Asbury Park, and how much she and Johnny loved living in the hotel. She went on for about twenty minutes.

Mayor Frank Fiorentino giving Johnny the Key to The City

ASBURY PARK WELCOMES
JOHNNY CASH
OCT. 18, 1985

My Dad the Night of his Banquet

Johnny later came back on stage and said, "I want to do a song and make a very special dedication. I don't know if you have been told tonight already, but it's a very special night for the Vaccaros. Twenty-five years ago tonight, Dr. Sebastian Vaccaro, Henry's father, was knighted by Pope John the XXIII. He was such a good man, and such a Godly man, that following this banquet when he accepted this honor, he got a call from the sick, and he went out after midnight and made house calls the night that he was knighted, and he died two days later."

"So for that very special person, the late Dr. Sebastian P. Vaccaro, for Henry, and for his mother, his sister, for the whole family, we want to do this song dedicated to people like him who have worked so hard and given so much with their hands." The band kicked in and the song went like this:

71

"These hands aren't the hands of gentlemen, these hands get calloused and old these hands raised a family; these hands built a home, now these hands raised to praise the Lord." I got chills when Johnny dedicated that song to my father. It came out of nowhere, so unexpected, and it really hit a nerve as I watched my mom, who was sitting in the front row, start to weep. My dad was special and so was Johnny Cash.

The shows were just spectacular, a real highlight of my life, to have my hero play my hometown for me! It just doesn't get any better than that and I will always cherish that evening.

Another thing about John and June when they came to town is how they interacted with people in and around the hotel, on the boardwalk downtown, and at local restaurants. They would stop and talk to anyone, allowing photographs and signing autographs; they had no problems with that at all. To me, all of that comes from upbringing and respect. They acted like plain common folks with no airs about them. It was not uncommon for both John and June to take walks on the boardwalk; A friend of mine told me how he was walking the boardwalk one cold day when two strangers approached him. The lady said hello and the man even tipped his hat, and it only hit him a few moments later that it was Johnny and June.

Johnny Saying Hello to Our Construction Crew at The Berkeley

Johnny and June at Mr. Peanut in Convention Hall

At One of my Construction Sites in Asbury Park

Walking Through Convention Hall

Inside Manny's 20' x 20' "Supermarket",
Manny offered Johnny a Special Price on Mangoes, $2 each or 2 for $5

And speaking of respect, it was on our first fishing trip to Bimini when Johnny asked for a phone, because he wanted to call his father. Back in the early '80s, there were no cell phones, and Bimini being an out-island in the Bahamian chain, had no direct phone cable linking it to the mainland. There was a "radio shack" with two phones, and only if the operator could get a clear signal were you able to make a call. The way it worked was very primitive, to say the least. The operator would dial in your number, which would be conveyed to Nassau over the air-waves. From there it would be transmitted through an underground cable to the States; some-times it worked other times not. I personally have waited several hours to make a call only to get cut off in the middle of a conversation that I couldn't hear anyway.

Well, I took Johnny up the little hill to the radio shack, located on the highest point on North Bimini just west of the King's Highway. Johnny gave the operator the number and by some strange luck it went through on the first try, and Johnny was now connected to his father. The two phone booths are not what we picture as a booth; they were nothing more than two wooden dividing walls separating each phone. There was one small shelf that the phone sat on, and if the call went through the operator would then ring your line. Well the phone rang in booth number two, and Johnny was now speaking to his father. Since there was no door on the booth, I could hear the conversation. But what I recall the most is the respect John had for his father and mother, as it was Yes, Daddy" or "Yes, sir" and "Yes ma'am" when he spoke to them. I felt a little uncomfortable so I stepped outside until the call was completed. Again, I must emphasize the humility that this man had, and how genuinely good he was.

As I have previously mentioned, June was a real businesswoman, and she knew how to capitalize on every asset, June wrote several books including a cookbook stocked full of the Carter Family's old recipes. When the hotel opened, we became famous for our fabulous Sunday Brunch, held in the Grand Foyer on the second level. On average, we would draw five hundred people or more. So one Sunday, the general manager decided to do a special brunch at the Berkeley Carteret Hotel that featured food from the recipes contained in June's cookbook, everything from homemade pies, cakes, puddings, cornbread and flapjacks to sausage and Southern ham were featured at this brunch. The icing on the cake happened when John, June, Helen and Anita Carter attended and explained each recipe to anyone who would ask. John and June sat at their own table, and would speak to everyone who came over to meet them. They were just real people, but they had a way of making everyone feel special.

Sunday Brunch at The Berkeley

Johnny, June, Me and Daughter Toni at Brunch

While at the hotel one day, John was approached by a gentleman from the Asbury Park chapter of the Veterans of Foreign Wars, VFW. He wanted to know if they could hold a ceremony for Missing in Action Veterans, MIA's who seemed to be forgotten, and would John possibly host it. Without hesitation, he emphatically said yes. So on October 28, 1988 in the Grand Foyer of the hotel, at least twenty members of the VFW Post 1333, including the Post Commander, honored Johnny Cash for his continued support of our military and his help for our MIAs.

The ceremony was scheduled for 2 PM. That morning I had arranged for a PA system along with a tape deck so we could play a recording of Johnny Cash singing "Ragged Old Flag" which was planned for at the conclusion of the event. Just prior to this affair, I informed Johnny

that everything was set with the tape and all that was required was for me to flip the switch when he was ready.

Johnny seemed a little taken back, maybe even slightly annoyed. He turned to me with his deep voice, and said, "We don't need any tape. I'm here, so why don't I do it live?" Needless to say, hearing Johnny Cash perform "Ragged Old Flag" live was beyond all expectations, and brought chills to those in attendance. John was presented with an MIA flag, and he immediately hoisted it on the flagpole at the main entrance of the Berkeley Carteret Hotel. That MIA flag flew proudly as long as we owned the hotel, as testament to our missing veterans and to Johnny's generosity and loyalty, can't say enough about that man. That's why he is, who he is Johnny Cash, The Man in Black.

Raising the POW MIA Flag at the Hotel

75

Chapter 12
Arthur "Guitar Boogie" Smith, Prelude to the Roast

It was now 1986 and our next fishing trip was planned for June. On July 6, 1986 Johnny was going to be roasted for a television show in Memphis, Tennessee, and the roast was going to be held at the Peabody Hotel. The Peabody is this magnificent classic Southern hotel; you have probably seen photos of its most famous guests, the family of five ducks that march from the elevator to the lobby twice a day on command. Quite a sight to see.

About three weeks before the roast, we were on Captain Jimmy's boat, the *Falcon,* somewhere off Bimini relaxing and dragging baits all over the gulfstream. John and I were just chatting when he asked, "Henry, you're going to be at my roast, aren't you?" I told him I wouldn't miss it for anything, and he began to tell me about his friend Arthur Smith, who would be in attendance. He said, "Arthur is an old Southern boy, and Arthur wrote the song 'The Fourth Man in the Fire' which I sing on stage, as well as 'Guitar Boogie.'"

I said, "I know the song, but I've never met Arthur." He said, "Well, he's going to be one of the roasters, so you will get a chance to meet each other at the Peabody. In the meantime I'm going to tell you a story about Arthur. Did you ever see that movie, *Deliverance*? Did you ever notice that song called 'Dueling Banjos'?"

I said, "Of course, it's the feature of the movie and then became a number-one country hit."

He said, "Arthur wrote that song, but the problem is when he wrote it, it had a different name. It was called 'Feudin' Banjos' and it never became popular, nor was it ever on any charts. It never went anywhere. But now somebody says, "Arthur you got to go see this movie *Deliverance*. I think that song you wrote is in that movie."

So now Johnny, who was now imitating Arthur, with his Southern drawl, said, "So Arthur goes to the movies and says, 'Damn, that's my song, and nobody's paying me any money.' Arthur went to an attorney, who asked, Arthur can you prove that you wrote the song, absolutely and he pulls out from his briefcase all the papers. The lawyer, after checking things out, said 'Arthur, you have the best case of copyright infringement that I have ever seen, well what do you mean. We'll sue them and you'll get triple damages, plus my legal fees. But if I were you, I wouldn't do a damn thing right now. Let it become a hit, and then we go after them. There's no risk because we've already got them, and you can prove you wrote the song.'"

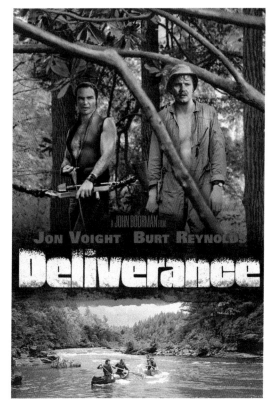

"So," Johnny continued, "the song 'Dueling Banjos' becomes the number-one country song in the nation. Arthur then makes a meeting with the vice president of Warner Brothers. By now Arthur feels that he doesn't need a lawyer, he's got all the legal advice he needed, so he just barged right into the VP's office." Now just picture Johnny imitating Arthur, with a real Southern drawl as he pretended to sit down at an imaginary executive's desk and said, "My *name* is Arthur Smith!, slams his fist down on the desk, he say, you boys done stole my song, and I wants my money, and I wants my money now!" I can't swear to those facts, but I can swear that's the story as told to me very animatedly by Johnny Cash.

Well after a little persuasion, Arthur gets his money, and he got a multimillion dollar out-of-court settlement, in what was, as it turned out, a landmark case on copyright infringement. *(one for the history books)* and that was my introduction to a man named Arthur Smith, via Johnny Cash.

The roast was scheduled to be in the Grand Ballroom of the Peabody Hotel in Mcmphis Tennessee, and there, Johnny was to receive the Shalom Peace Award, from the State of Israel, and The National Jewish Fund. Johnny had made a movie in Israel called *Gospel Road*, about the life of Christ, and he gave some of the proceeds to the State of Israel for letting him make the movie, and then allowed the Billy Graham Organization to distribute the movie and profit from its viewing. The Shalom Peace Award was given for Johnny's humanitarian deeds. The city of Memphis was chosen, as Johnny got his start at the Sun Recording Studio in Memphis.

There was only one direct flight from the New York area to Memphis, so my secretary reserved me a seat in the first-class cabin. That flight departed

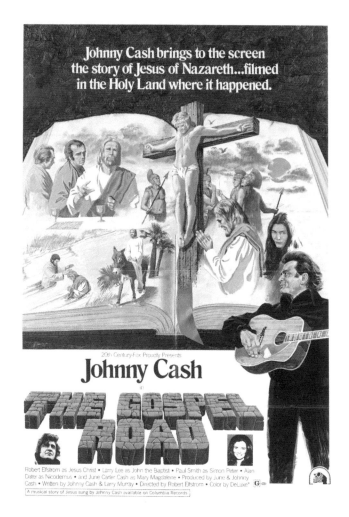

Years Later, Waylon Playing One of My Vaccaro Guitars

from LaGuardia and got us into Memphis at about 9:30 in the morning, which was one hour behind New York. After boarding the plane, who did I spot in the last row of the first class cabin but Waylon Jennings and his road manager David Trask. I had known and befriended Waylon from being around John, as we had been introduced to each other several years prior.

There were a few empty seats between Waylon and myself, and after the flight took off, Waylon looked up and said, "Henry is that you? Come on back here with us." So I walked back and took this empty seat just in front of him. Waylon said, "Boy, we are going to have a good old time with this roast. I'm in charge of this, and this is the first time I've been in charge of anything in my life." (These comments, appropriately, were made shortly after Waylon kicked his million-dollars-a-year cocaine habit.)

78

He leaned over and asked, "Did you ever meet John J Hooker?"

I said, "No, I don't know who John J Hooker is."

So, he turned and pointed to a gentleman sitting a couple of seats up. He said, "John J, come here, I want you to meet Henry, and we are all going to have a good ol' time at this roast." That was my formal introduction to the legendary career politician named John J Hooker.

John J Hooker was a classy man, back then, very handsome; about six foot two, with wavy white hair. His trademark was a three-piece suit and a gold-handled walking stick, and sometimes he wore a derby. John J was a politician's politician; he ran for Governor of Tennessee two or three times, and he lost two or three times. He was also the former President of STP Oil Company, and I believe the former President of United Press International.

I was impressed with this elite

John J Hooker

Waylon and his Son Shooter Years Later at John Carter's Wedding

gentleman that I was going to share the dais with. After landing in Memphis, we all got off the plane and Waylon said "I've got a limo; I'll take all of you to the hotel."

We got in the car, and I'm sitting in the back with Waylon, and out of the clear blue sky he started telling me about how he kicked his cocaine habit, and how he wanted the world to know, and that's why he was telling me and anyone else who would listen. He said, "I bought this place out in Arizona, and we'd just had a little son named Shooter, and I knew I was going to kill myself unless I got off this damn cocaine, so I just went cold turkey. Damn tough, but I'm proud of what I did; that's why I can now say that I'm in charge of this

79

thing tonight." This is the first time I've been in charge of anything in a long time."

We got to the hotel probably around 10:30 or so in the morning, and we had the whole day to kill because the roast wasn't until seven o'clock that night. So I turned to John J and then to Waylon and said, "Have you guys ever been to Graceland? I'd love to go, and we have all afternoon." So Waylon said, "Hell, I've been there plenty of times; me and Elvis was good friends." just like that, me and Elvis was good friends, so I looked at John J and I said, "How about you?" He says "Let's go." Waylon's road manager, David Trask says, "Hey I'd like to go too." So we agreed that after we checked in at the Peabody we'd all meet in the lobby and take a taxi over to Graceland.

Graceland

After we actually got to view Graceland, though, I was kind of disappointed. I mean, after being to Johnny Cash's house, Graceland looked like a farmhouse. It was set very close to the road, and surrounded by a typical housing development. It seemed to be one big tourist attraction, but I still wanted to go inside. In order to get into Graceland, you have to first check in and buy a ticket at the welcome center located on the opposite side of the highway, and then wait in line for a tram to take you across the street and up the driveway to the main entrance. While waiting for the tram you could buy a ticket and go into Elvis's airplane and his tour bus, as well as browse through the souvenir shop. Our problem was that there was a four-hour wait to get on the tram to actually see Elvis's home.

This was the Thursday of the 4th of July weekend, so Graceland was packed with tourists and we didn't have all that much time to waste. So I turned to John J and said, "I don't want to wait for four hours; you're a big shot. Get us in." The next thing I knew, John J Hooker called up the Governor's office and within fifteen minutes a private van pulled up, a tour guide came over and instructed us to get in, and off we went to Graceland. All of us, John J his traveling secretary, David Trask, and myself with our own personal guide for a VIP tour. We were driven past all the trams right to the front door; our guide escorted us in front of all the visitors who were waiting in line at the main entrance. We were personally guided through the house, even to the upstairs level that is off limits to the average tourist. The tour ended up at the gravesites of Elvis and his mother and father. So folks, that's how I came to know and realize that John J Hooker was the real deal. If you met him, you too would feel the same way, and love the guy.

Chapter 13

The Good Ol' Boys and Me Roast Johnny

Johnny's roast at the famed Peabody Hotel in Memphis, Tennessee was a black-tie affair as Johnny Cash is set to receive the Shalom Peace Award from the Jewish National Fund for Johnny's work toward world peace. Naturally this is a sold out affair with well over 600 or 700 guests in attendance at the Grand Ballroom they included, the Governor of Tennessee, Senators, Congressman and other dignitaries from both the political and entertainment world, members of the Jewish community, and just plain folk like me.

Things got started off with a cocktail reception where John and June mingled with the crowd, posed for photos and signed a few autographs. Soon the lights dimmed to signal the start of the formal dinner and the roast. Do any of you remember the old Dean Martin roasts that were on TV, packed with some of the greats of the entertainment world? This was similar, except that this dais was full of the greats of country music—and me. The setting, a low stage that was used as a dais, was set some two or three feet higher than the main floor. In the center was a podium about chest high with a microphone.

Just to the left sat Waylon Jennings, the Master of Ceremonies who said "I ain't never wore one of these monkey suit before, and I'm only doing it because of John." Next to Waylon sat his wife Jessi Colter, actor John Schneider, Rick Blackburn, the President of CBS Records in Nashville, then-record producer Chips Moman, and the legendary Sam Phillips. To the right of the podium sat Johnny Cash, June Carter Cash, John Carter, singer-songwriter Jeannie C. Riley, Kris and Lisa Kristofferson, Arthur Smith, myself and John J Hooker. Sitting directly behind the

roasters were two tiers of other dignitaries.

So, now to the Roast, it's show time. The first roaster is a man named Sam Phillips, and anybody who knows anything about the birth of rock and roll and the evolution of country music knows that name, like an opera fan would know the name Pavarotti. Sam Phillips owned a little recording studio, located on Union Avenue in Memphis Tennessee in the 1950s named Sun Studios. At one time he had under contract Elvis Presley, Johnny Cash, Carl Perkins, Jerry Lee Lewis, Roy Orbison, Charlie Rich and a stable other artists. Most people agree that the birth of rock and roll and rockabilly all started at tiny Sun Records.

It is now time to hear from the legendary Sam Phillips. I did not recognize Sam at first, as he had a full growth of beard and long hair. As Sam approached the microphone, he seemed real nervous, like maybe he was stoned out of his mind kind of nervous. When he finally started talking it seemed like one word ran into the other and you couldn't even understand him. For the folks who don't know this, Sam is the guy who sold Elvis Presley's contract to RCA. The deal was arranged by Colonel Tom Parker for $35,000 dollars plus the back royalties that he owed of $5,000 dollars. So with that background, I guess Sam had every right to be stoned.

In fact, several weeks earlier, while in Bimini, John and I were discussing Sam Phillips and his early days recording for Sam. I asked John, "How come you left Sun Records? That's where you got your start; he gave you your first big break."

"I would probably still be at Sun," said John, "except for one major problem: that damn Sam Phillips couldn't count. My first royalty check was like $2.41 from

Sam Phillips

"Hey Porter." he forgot how to count or was hiding the money that's the main reason why I left."

Johnny said, he also told me that he earned only about $6,000 in royalties from "Folsom Prison Blues."

So, now we have a wacked-out Sam Phillips who was so incoherent that Waylon gonged him and then looked for the hook to get him away from the microphone. Kris Kristofferson then

Waylon, John and I, Years Later

grabbed the microphone and said "Ladies and gentleman, just think of this: the birth of rock n roll started under the tutelage of the guys at Sun Studios and this man was their leader. Boy, God sure does things in mysterious ways." That brought a laugh from the audience.

I was the next roaster, and I was a nervous wreck. I rarely ever drink, but I quickly downed three scotches, as I needed some bottled courage. Now, it's my, turn after the embarrassment that I had just witnessed, I was scared to death to speak to a now-irritated crowd of over 600 people. But I stood up and walked to the dais. Adjusted the microphone and let it go. That night is still very vivid in my mind, for it was one of the highlights of my life, and I remember this as if it was only yesterday. I started to read a phony telegram that I created on the airplane en route to Memphis. It went something like this: "Ladies and gentlemen, I have the honor of reading a telegram from a former President and very close friend of Johnny and June." Everybody was milling around, thinking it was President Carter that I was referring to, because I believe June was a distant cousin of Jimmy Carter. I continued, "Mr. J.R. Cash, Peabody Hotel, Memphis, Tennessee. Dear Johnny, congratulations on this momentous occasion. Your life is truly an inspiration to all who know you. I am sorry, but pressing business keeps me out of the country. I hope to see you at the bank in Switzerland. Signed, your friend, President Ferdinand Marcos."

So with everybody laughing I started to feel a bit more comfortable and now had the guts to drop a bomb (remember now, this is in front of a large Jewish audience). I stood up tall with my reading glasses on, and said, "You know folks, while everybody is in such a good mood I am going to tell you something that only a few of his closest friends know." I said, to a crowd that was listening intently, "Johnny Cash is only his stage name; his real name is Murray Lipchitz, the only son of Ida and Izzy Lipchitz, and when they landed on Ellis Island they sold the Statue of Liberty for cash and changed their name." I thought I might have laid a bomb, but instead the place went nuts and exploded with laughter, especially the Jewish audience. Now Kris Kristofferson grabbed the mike, turned to Johnny and said, "Son, you come a long way from a boy named Sue to Murray Lipchitz." Again the audience laughed uncontrollably.

That episode was hard to top but I followed up with, "Life wasn't easy for young John. His father took him out into the woods, but he didn't take him far enough, and so he found his way back home." I continued by saying, "Everybody who has ever been to Johnny's house knows that he is an avid antique collector, he has a wonderful collection of Louis XIV furniture, but if he doesn't pay Louie by the fourteenth, he has got to give it all back." Those jokes also brought laughter from the audience. I was so happy as I returned to my seat, that I didn't screw up with my few jokes.

Well, the next roaster was none other than Arthur "Guitar Boogie" Smith, the songwriter that Johnny talked about in his conversation with me several weeks earlier while fishing in Bimini. (*You can recall Arthur wrote "Dueling Banjos" the number one hit song from the movie "Deliverance"*) Arthur, a man in his seventies, turned out to be a real character. He strolled to the dais and proceeded to tell a few stories about Waylon and Johnny: "Now let me give you a little bit of background. It was in the early '60s when Johnny and Waylon Jennings lived together in an apartment that they rented in Nashville, and there is nothing that those two country boys didn't do back then, that these rockers do today.

In fact they probably blazed the trail for what some of today's stars do with booze, pills, womanizing, tearing up hotel rooms, etcetera—they did it all.

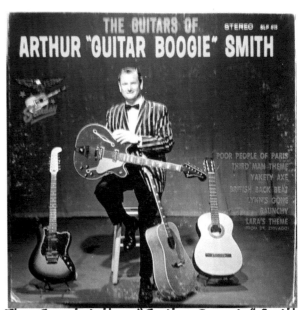

The Great Arthur "Guitar Boogie" Smith

You have to hear Arthur, in his deep Southern accent, as he enunciated certain words. (Like the word siren, by pronouncing it as *sireeen*, and *flashing* pronounced *flashin*) Arthur now starts his monologue by saying, "Ladies and gentlemen, I knew Johnny and Waylon way back then, but it was in that nervous period in their life that Johnny comes over to my house one day and my wife Dorothy was sewing on the machine and the thread come a' loose. Johnny says 'don't worry about it Arthur,' and I'll be darned he threaded it while it was still moving." Arthur was making a rapid up-and-down shaking movement with his right hand, pretending to hold a thread in it. Arthur then proceeded to tell a story about a movie that Johnny was once making.

"Johnny invited me down to the set, where he was playing the part of a Catholic Priest in this movie. At the end of the day's shooting Johnny says 'Arthur I'll drive you back to the hotel and we'll get something to eat. I get in the car, Johnny's driving and he is all over the road. (*It must have still been in that nervous period in his life*). The next thing I know, a policeman pulls up beside us with the blue light flashin', rings the *sireeen* and the boy pulls us over. (*Arthur is now making a cranking motion with his right hand like winding up the siren*) The policeman walks over to the car and looks down at Johnny, sitting behind the steering wheel who is still

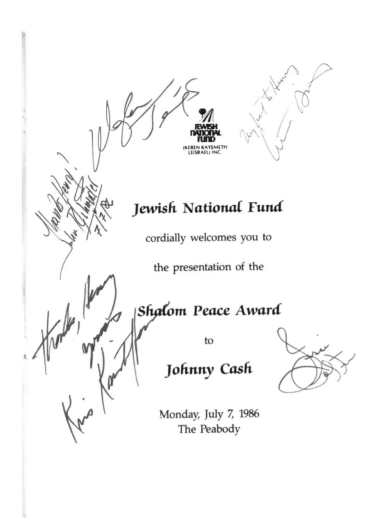

Jewish National Fund

cordially welcomes you to

the presentation of the

Shalom Peace Award

to

Johnny Cash

Monday, July 7, 1986
The Peabody

wearing the clerical collar and says, 'Father is there something wrong?' Johnny says 'I don't think so son, I am just a little tired and we are driving back to the hotel.'

The police officer turns around and is ready to leave but out of the corner of his eye spots a bottle in the front seat. He says 'Why Father what's in that bottle sitting on the seat between you and that other gentleman? Johnny says, 'Oh that's only holy water.' The police officer reaches in the car, takes out the bottle, unscrews the cap, puts his finger into the liquid, and proceeds to taste it. The officer then says 'Father, that's wine!' Johnny looked at him and looked up to heaven as he raised and spread both his hands and said, 'Praise the Lord; He did it again!'" The house again broke down in laughter.

The next roaster turned out to be none other than John J Hooker. The man who ran for Governor of Tennessee twice and lost both times. John J missed his profession, as I believe he was born to be a comic. All 6'3" of John J stood up at the dais like an orchestra leader in complete command of the orchestra. He said, "Ladies and gentlemen, I love politics and I love the people. But when you have run for statewide office and lost as many times as I have lost you learn one thing: work the other guy's crowd. While you are here waiting for Johnny Cash to do something and I'm talking, you've got to listen to me. You folks don't understand: here I am, a grown man, pregnant with not one but two acceptance speeches undelivered." At this point, Waylon looked over at John J bewildered, while John J used both hands to pat his gut and went on to say, "We are all in the presence of the king. Johnny Cash thinks he was born in a manger, not *the* manger but *any* manger." John J then turned left and looked down at Johnny. "How do you think I feel? Every time I turn on that damn television set and see you, you say 'Hello I'm Johnny Cash.' Well who the hell do you think I think you are? You ain't Waylon Jennings. You ain't Kris Kristofferson, I *know* you're Johnny Cash. I feel like saying 'Well hello, I am John J Hooker." More laughter, of course. He closed by saying, "Johnny, I am here to honor and salute you, sir, for you are a real man."

PROGRAM

INTRODUCTION OF DAIS

WAYLON JENNINGS
MASTER OF CEREMONIES

INVOCATION
RABBI RAPHAEL GROSSMAN

DINNER

WELCOME AND ACKNOWLEDGEMENTS
NOREEN FREIDEN, PRESIDENT
MEMPHIS JNF COUNCIL

TRIBUTE ROAST
WAYLON JENNINGS
MASTER OF CEREMONIES

Sam Phillips	Arthur Smith	Jessi Colter
Jerry Lee Lewis	Rick Blackburn	John Jay Hooker
Carl Perkins	Joe Cates	June Carter Cash
Steve Cropper	Paul Richey	Henry V. Vaccaro
Tony Joe White	Jeannie C. Riley	
Chips Moman	John Schneider	

PRESENTATION OF SHALOM AWARD
DR. SAMUEL I. COHEN, EXEC. VP
JNF OF AMERICA

ACCEPTANCE
JOHNNY CASH

SHOWCASE OF MEMPHIS MUSIC
JOHNNY CASH, PRESENTOR

BENEDICTION
REV. FLOYD GRESSETT

The show had many other roasters, and it including June Carter Cash, Rick Blackburn, Chips Moman, Jeannie C. Riley, Jessi Colter, and John Schneider. The roast ended with a moving tribute song written and sung by Kris Kristofferson that cast a true light on this incredible man. John R. Cash that we are all honoring this very night. It was called "Good Morning, John" and went just like this...

Kris, Me and John Years Later

Good morning, John; Ain't it great to see your future
shining brighter than the naked light of day.
You made it son, but I confess there was a time or two,
I thought you might let it slip away.
I love you, John, in the cold and holy darkness you
were always shining brighter than a star. God bless
you, John, for the love and joy you've given and the
living inspiration that you are.
You scared me, John, because you crossed so many
borders in danger with a price upon your head.
They got you, John, and it hurt to see so many friends
who ran along beside you lying dead.
I know you, John; there ain't nothing you can't handle
now 'cause there ain't nothing bigger than your heart.
Keep shining, John, for you were to others in the dark
and holy wonder that you are.
Hang in there, John; it's a rocky road to glory but the
straight and strongest will survive.
Keep smiling, John, we won't make it there tomorrow,
but today let's say we're lucky we're alive.
I'll see you, John, though the best of good intentions
have a way of getting scattered by the wind.
I mean it, John, you can lose your mind and memory
but you aren't going to lose me as your friend.......
Kris Kristofferson

"Needless to say, the night of John's roast was filled with stars, laugher, and tears and Henry Vaccaro from small town Asbury Park, New Jersey was blessed to be there.

Chapter 14

The Man Comes Around Praying For My Dying Mom

Three Angels From Heaven

This Next Johnny Cash Story is For You Mom

I have casually mentioned my mother in some previous stories. After God created mothers and my mom, he threw the mold away. I really don't know where to start, so I'll start way back when my mom, Rosemarie Huhn Vaccaro, raised four children. I'm the oldest, along with my two sisters Frances and Rosemarie, and my younger brother Sebastian. My mother was born in Long Branch, New Jersey but spent most of her childhood in Asbury Park. Mom held a summer and after-school job in a candy shop on the boardwalk to earn money to fulfill her dream of becoming a registered nurse.

Her parents were of German descent, and her father's name was Henry Huhn; her mother was Anna. After nursing school she worked for Dr. Otto Holters, MD, a prominent surgeon with offices in Asbury Park. That is where she met and fell in love with my father, Sebastian P. Vaccaro MD, whose parents were of Italian descent. His parents were Henry and Annunziata Vaccaro, so you can see how I got the name Henry. It was a relatively simple choice, no fighting over that one, since both grandfathers had the same first name.

Shortly After I Was Born

My mother was always there for us kids. She made sure that we lacked nothing. Holidays were very special, as was each child's birthday. In retrospect I don't know how she did it; after all she worked for my father as a nurse, and he would burn through nurses like Grant took Richmond. My father was a maverick as far as doctors go, he never took a day off except a two-week Florida vacation, and had office hours seven days a week and house calls each night. *I didn't make a mistake that was not a typo Monday thru Saturday 9 to 12 am, 2 to 5 pm, 7 to 9 pm, Sunday was different only afternoon hours 1 to 5 pm, house calls every night.*) Because my Father had a hard time keeping nurses (I *wonder why)* Mom would work every night, usually until midnight even going on house calls with him.

My sister Fran and I were born at 509 Fourth Avenue, Asbury Park in an apartment over my father's office. In 1946 we moved into a magnificent estate type home in the neighboring community of Interlaken, New Jersey, about two miles from his office. My sister Rosemarie, or "Roe" as she liked to be called and my brother Sebastian were born in our new home. As kids we had everything you could dream of: the first in-ground swimming pool in town, a shuffleboard court, gas powered miniature cars to run all over with, and most of all we had a loving mother and father. Our only problem was we rarely saw them.

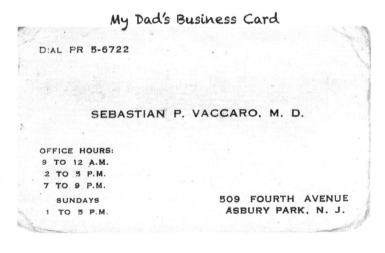

My Dad's Business Card

DIAL PR 5-6722

SEBASTIAN P. VACCARO, M. D.

OFFICE HOURS:
9 TO 12 A.M.
2 TO 5 P.M.
7 TO 9 P.M.
SUNDAYS
1 TO 5 P.M.

509 FOURTH AVENUE
ASBURY PARK, N. J.

We couldn't wait until suppertime at 5 o'clock, when daddy would come home. We always ate together as a family. Mom sometimes had the day off from the office but that didn't mean she wasn't working. You see my father was a genius when it came to real estate, too; he purchased or at one time owned five large apartment houses, two beachfront parking lots and maybe 10 to 15 other income-producing properties. And who do you think managed them? None other than Rosemarie H. Vaccaro. Thinking back, not many people that I know could have handled that workload, but mom seldom complained, for a day off was not in her vocabulary either.

In seventh and eighth grade I went off to military school, Bordentown Military Institute, located in Bordentown New Jersey, a good hours drive from home. And who do you think drove me back and forth at least twice a month? You guessed it again: mom.

My mom was always by my father's side, our lives all changed forever when my father died of a massive heart attack on October 21, 1959. We were all still in school, I was just starting my second year at Villanova University, and the other kids were still in high school. Mom was there, steady as the Rock of Gibraltar. She saw to it that we were all taken care of and maintained our lifestyle from the rental income of the various buildings that my father left for us, almost as if he knew that he wouldn't be around.

Mom had gotten her first introduction to Johnny Cash's music from the stereo that blasted throughout the house. In later years, I would take her to his concerts, especially at the Garden State Arts Center where we had box seats. She was with me the first time I met John, in fact, at a reception backstage at the Arts Center in 1973, and she really liked him. Several years later, young John Carter would come over to her house with Henry Jr. to go in the swimming pool and sometime spent the night..

Johnny's First Meeting wit the Vaccaro Clan

By 1985, Johnny and June were spending more and more time in Asbury Park at the Berkeley Carteret Hotel. On more than one occasion, June would come over to spend an afternoon with mom just sitting around the pool like two peas in a pod. Anytime the Johnny Cash Show was on the east coast, my mother had a standing invitation from Johnny to attend the show and go backstage.

Ten years earlier my mom had developed breast cancer, and by late 1986 and 1987 it was getting worse. By January 1987 she was bedridden, and we were looking for someone to take care of her. God does things in strange ways, and he sent us an angel from heaven. This angel had a name, Evelyn Middleton, RN. Perhaps not so coincidentally, when Evelyn was a teenager still going to high school, my father had brought her into our home to live and gradually, with my mom's help, they trained her into becoming a nurse.

There is a lot more, Evelyn was a light-skinned black girl; her father was black and her mom white. She had eight or nine brothers and sisters, and they were all very poor and lived in a small rented house on the west side of the tracks. My father was their family doctor, Evelyn's maiden name was Garrett, and her Father was a hard worker and worked for a coal company but just barely earned enough to subsist. My mom saw Evelyn's potential and knew that she had to get out of that environment to survive.

As mentioned, we had a very large home, so she moved in on the third floor. Evelyn went to St. Rose High School in the borough of Belmar, some six miles from our home, which meant that she had to get up very early in the morning and walk a mile to the bus stop just to pursue her education. She finished high school and went into nursing training, all the time working part time at my father's office. After my father died, she then went to work for my uncle, Dr. Henry J. Vaccaro, MD. Evelyn left after he stopped practicing medicine, and soon we lost track of her. But my mom got sick and many years later, out of the clear blue sky as if sent by God; Evelyn shows up to take care of her, right until the end. Evelyn knows how we feel about her; we love her as part of our family.

Evelyn with Johnny and June

I believe it was April of 1987, and my beautiful daughter Toni (my mom's first grandchild) is going to be married in the Crystal Ballroom of the Berkeley Carteret Hotel. Mom was really ill by now, and one of her last wishes was to go to Toni's wedding that Sunday night at the hotel. She had not been out of her bed in over a week and we never even thought she could make the wedding. On Saturday morning, April 20, 1987, God sent his next two angels. They also had names: John R. Cash and June Carter Cash. Johnny and June arrived at our home to see my mom; Evelyn met them at the door and escorted them upstairs to her bedroom. I was in the other room when Evelyn called me in, as John wanted to pray for my Mother.

John knelt down on the floor at mom's right while June knelt down at her left. John placed his left hand on Mother's forehead and with his right hand clasped her right hand. June, on the other side, reached across the bed to hold mom's left hand and they both prayed to God, for my mother to be out of pain and have the strength to attend Toni's wedding, which was the next evening

Well the hand of God and the hands of the Cash's were at work. Mom had a peaceful night, the next afternoon Evelyn dressed her, put her in a wheelchair and wrapped her favorite fox stole across her frail body. Johnny had sent a car over to drive mom and Evelyn to the reception, where he and June were awaiting their arrival. John helped her from the car into the wheelchair

and then proceeded, with June at his side, to push her into the elevator up to the Crystal Ballroom where the reception was being held. They sat with her the entire night until she got tired and had to go home.

Mom got such an uplift from attending the affair that she started to feel a little better, but it was only a false hope, as my beautiful mother, Rosemarie Huhn Vaccaro, passed away on May 31, 1987. And Johnny, the amazing and respectful man he was, cancelled a concert so he and June could attend her funeral.

How did I do Mom?

Johnny, My Mom and June at
My Daughter's Wedding

92

Chapter 15   "Stuff"

This and That...Stories and Tidbits

While traveling on the tour bus with Johnny and June, if anybody got hungry June would make up a concoction of anything that was leftover in the refrigerator, put it in a frying pan, sprinkle some cheese on top and then stick it in the oven. What came out she simply called "stuff." Since this chapter contains a little of this and a little of that, in deference to June, this chapter is also simply called "Stuff."

It's Called Humility

Over the years I have met and gotten to know many so-called celebrities through my involvement with the Kramer Guitar Company, from the likes of Jon Bon Jovi, Kenny Rogers, Hank Jr., Willie Nelson, Kris Kristofferson, Waylon, Gene Simmons, Dee Snider, Eddie Van Halen and even John McEnroe, etc. What separates Johnny Cash from all the rest is one simple word: *humility*? Johnny never forgot where he came from. His father, Ray Cash, who lived across the street from Johnny's home on Caudill Drive in Hendersonville, Tennessee, had planted a cotton bush in his front yard to remind himself and others where he came from. When Johnny would address his parents it was always yes sir or yes ma'am one quick story for a reality check.

Too Big For Your Britches

In the late sixties, Johnny Cash had the number-one record, the number-one album, the number-one TV show, on the cover of *Life magazine* and was the biggest record seller ever for Columbia Records. At that time, he was asked to host a benefit show for a charity that Mamie Eisenhower was involved with. The show was held at the Waldorf Astoria in New York City and was a thousand-dollar-a table dinner attended to by the likes of Gene Autry, Bing Crosby and Raquel Welch.

June described the following scene to me. Johnny had just mounted the stage right after introducing Raquel Welch to the audience, and he seemed all smitten. He was wearing his Andrew Jackson boots laced to his knees, tight black jodhpurs, and his trademark preacher jacket. Bob Wootton kicked off "Folsom Prison Blues" and Johnny reached for his guitar pick but dropped it on the floor. As he bent over, his pants tore, they didn't just tear, but they *ripped*— from one side to the other, exposing his pink legs.

To hide his embarrassment, he lowered the guitar that he was playing to cover up his problem. After the song, he rushed off stage into the dressing room and (according to June) he was furious and outraged and no one could talk to him for quite a while. After things calmed down, June made a classic statement that only she could make: "*John, the Good Lord was just sending you a message: you're getting too big for your britches.*" Folks the story *must* be true, as that wonderful June Carter Cash told it to me.

JC Unit One

The Johnny Cash Show used the Berkeley Carteret Hotel as a base for all their shows on the east coast that were within driving distance of the hotel. On one particular day, Johnny's tour bus pulled up to the front door of the hotel where he, June, John Carter, Helen, Anita and myself stepped on board for the two-hour drive to a concert in a small club on the outskirts of Philadelphia. The guys in the band had departed earlier in the day by car, as well as Johnny's Peterbilt tractor pulling that 48-foot trailer full of all the sound equipment, instruments, lighting, sound board, piano and stage props. Johnny's tour bus was an MCI coach shell with a custom-designed interior built by the Executive Coach Company of Columbus, Ohio. It included a stateroom for John as well as a kitchen, a dressing room and a rest area for June.

The exterior was polished chrome with wide black, white, and silver stripes running down the entire length beneath the dark charcoal gray windows that permitted the passengers to see out while the public could not see in. There was a very simple designation painted in six-inch high white letters on the lower black stripe at the rear of the coach: *JC UNIT ONE*. The Tennessee license plate was simply *MUSIC 1*.

We arrived at the tiny club, which only held about 800 people, around 7 o'clock for the 8 o'clock show since this was a smaller club it did not have large dressing rooms the bus was used for that purpose by John and June. Helen and Anita used the dressing room inside the club, as did John Carter and the band members. The stage crew, headed by Jay Dauro from Huntsville, Alabama, had everything set up including the sound check. So when it was show time, everything was ready.

The show went off without a hitch, but John Carter only got a lukewarm reception as he performed several songs he had written. I don't think it was the songs so much as the crowd had come to hear Johnny Cash and anything less than that was not what they wanted.

(I have to mention how very proud I am of John Carter, whom I have known since he was seven years old: he has truly come into his own as a father, songwriter, producer, author, etc. He has grown into a wonderful man, that his mother and father would be so proud of.)

After the show, we all got on the bus for the ride back to Asbury Park. Bob Wootton, W.S. Holland and the other guys in the band headed to the next venue, which was in Allentown, Penn-

sylvania, with the Peterbilt to follow after it had been loaded. On the ride back to the hotel, Johnny called me into his stateroom to chat. As we were talking, Johnny looked out the window on his left and spotted the Spectrum, which held 16,000 people. John said, "You know, Henry, I used to sell out that place, this is after playing to an audience of maybe 700 people. It really can be a downer but I can handle it: as long as just one person enjoyed my music tonight in that little club, that's all that mattered."

Roasted Peppers and Mozzarella
The John Piancione Story

When I look back to the start of my friendship with Johnny Cash, I think much of it was really nurtured through his stomach. I know you think that is a crazy comment but it's true .It probably started in the late '70s, when I would have this incredible opportunity to get on his bus with Bob Wootton leading the way and would spend a few minutes with John and June before they would depart for the next show. During those early times, I noticed that John would usually sit down at the small banquet table in his private compartment, grab a soda and ask June to make a sandwich from the kitchen, which was located just to the rear. This was his quiet time, and after coming down from a natural high due to being on stage performing, he would eat.

In the early '80s, John and June sublet an apartment on Central Park South in New York City from Liza Minnelli. Whenever I was invited to the apartment, instead of bringing a small

95

gift I would stop at a restaurant near my home called Mom's Kitchen, an Italian establishment owned forever by the Aldarelli Family. So you know the food must be good, I would order large portions of their specialties. One was giambotta, a concoction of sausage, chicken, peppers, onions and potatoes all sautéed together in a light wine sauce, and the other was their homemade ravioli. John loved Italian food, and as I soon learned, you could not find real Italian food in Tennessee. As our friendship really started to develop, I would quite often go on short five or six-day tours with them.

There was also a fabulous Italian deli in Bradley Beach, New Jersey, a couple towns over from Asbury Park, called Piancione's. My father first took us there in 1957, when it originally opened for business. It was located in the middle of town on Main Street, and you could smell this place from blocks away. Giant six-foot hunks of provolone cheese and salami hung from the ceiling, homemade sausage and fresh mozzarella filled the showcase, where there was also every type of cold cut: salami, capicola (round hot ham with a red pepper crust), prosciuttini (rectangular shaped ham with black peppercorn crust), prosciutto, (prosciutto di Parma, the finest cured ham in the world), and soppressata (very hot and round in shape) all on display. Now add to that the aroma of fresh baked bread: it was overwhelming.

John and June Enjoying Some of Piancione's Finest

I figured that since I knew how much Johnny and June loved Italian food, it was time to get them addicted to the real stuff. I purchased a small portable cooler and packed it full of everything that Piancione's had to offer, including a variety of homemade breads containing cheese, sausage, and other types of meat. Needless to say, when I would bring it on the bus I was the hit of the show. Well, not me, but the food. Later, I would even bring Piancione's food on our fishing trips to the Bahamas.

In 1985, John and June had settled into their apartment at the Berkeley Carteret Hotel, as they had given up the one in New York City. Both John and June had heard so much about Piancione's deli and my stories about

this little old Italian man John Piancione, who would get up at 2 a.m. every morning and go to the deli just to make the fresh bread for that day's consumption, that they wanted to meet him. So for the next several years when they were in Asbury Park we would always drop by to see Mr. Piancione, his wife Ethel, their sons John and Chip and their daughter, who all worked the business. Sometimes when the Cash's would head back to Nashville they would stock up with a month's

Me, Mr. Piancione and June at the Piancione Store

supply of food. And on several occasions Piancione's would send food by Federal Express, packed in dry ice, to their home in Hendersonville, Tennessee.

I believe it was in 1992, after returning from a European tour, that John and June decided to rest up at the Berkeley Carteret for a week or so before heading home. Johnny called me and wanted go to Piancione's for lunch, because he had a special gift for John. When we arrived, Ethel said her husband was in the hospital with a serious wound on his leg that won't heal and it might have to be amputated. John Piancione, we knew, had sugar diabetes real bad, as a result the wound on his leg was not healing his other leg had already been amputated and replaced with a wooden prosthesis. Johnny did not hesitate and says to me "Henry how far is the hospital?" "John it's about 5 miles away " "We have to go there." Of course, we got into my car and headed toward Jersey Shore Medical Center in Neptune, after parking, it's into the main lobby and the information desk. I asked for John Piancione's room number.

When we arrive, Johnny Cash was immediately recognized and a nurse personally escorted us to John's room. The door was open, but no John Piancione. The nurse checked at the nurses' station only to be told that he was receiving treatment in some type of oxygen chamber on a lower floor. The nurse received permission allowing us to visit him in this special room, and upon entering, Mr. Piancione could not believe his eyes; Johnny Cash embraced him.

John asked what's wrong (In broken English, John Piancione said, "They wanna cutta off my otter leg, an I no wanna dem do dat."

How come? John asked; (Dis sore she no wanna getta better) Johnny reached into the bag he was carrying and gave John a crucifix that was blessed by the Pope; he had brought it all the way from the Vatican especially for John Piancione, unaware that he was sick and in the hospital. And you know what, folks? The doctors never had to amputate John's other leg. John Piancione died peacefully about three years ago and at the viewing that crucifix was proudly resting alongside him in the coffin. His wife Ethel said that cross-meant so much to him that's where he would have wanted it displayed. *THE POWER OF PRAYER!*

A Ray Cash Story

This is a story that John told me on one of our fishing trips while we were having a little quiet time, on Captain Jimmy's boat as we were trolling baits in the clear water off the tiny island of Cat Cay in the Bahamas. We were looking for that elusive blue marlin and were fishing with freshly caught mackerel caught the day before. John was telling me about his dad, Ray Cash, who had recently passed away on December 23, 1985. He told me a couple of interesting stories. Ray lived with his wife Carrie in a ranch house that John had purchased for them and which sat almost directly across from Johnny's house on Caudill Drive, in Hendersonville, Tennessee.

John's mother would never allow Ray's dog Snowball in the house, but as he was dying he whispered to Carrie "Could you please let the dog in the house when the weather gets bad?"

On another occasion while Ray was in the hospital, John went to see him, after a day's filming of a TV movie called *The Last Days of Frank and Jesse James*. It was shot in and around the Nashville area. Johnny Cash played the part of Frank James; Kris Kristofferson played Jesse James. June Carter Cash, Ed Bruce and David Allen Coe were also in the film. While in the hospital, Ray asked Johnny what was going on in the movie.

"Daddy, I'm in this movie playing the part of Frank James and today was the last day for me because I just died."

"What day did you die, son?" Ray asked.

"February 15, 1915."

Ray looked at Johnny and thought for a few moments, before saying, "No, I think Frank died on February 18, 1915. I remember it was when I was stationed at Fort Hood in Texas and we lowered the flag to half-staff for Frank James."

Well, Johnny went back and checked it out: the movie script had the date wrong, and Ray Cash had it right.

Johnny's Parents, Carrie and Ray Cash
Photo Courtesy of Kelly Hancock

When Mr. Ray Cash passed away on December 23, 1985, June called me to inform me of his passing. I asked her for the date and time of the funeral, which she gave me. I don't recall the actual date now, whether it was the 27th or 28th, but I knew it was my place to be there. I have a friend, Marc Nelson, who also knew Johnny and he asked if he could go with me. We both flew into Nashville where we were met at the airport by Johnny's Security Chief, Armando, who picked us up in June's black Mercedes and drove us to John's home. Once in Johnny's home we gathered around, and paid our respects. Waylon Jennings stopped in to offer his condolences as well. John had arranged for all of us to travel to the church by limo and we awaited that arrival.

The funeral service was held at the Baptist church in Hendersonville. It was a beautiful service, and Johnny insisted we sit up front with the family. What I remember most was Connie Smith signing "The Tennessee Waltz," as I later learned that was Ray Cash's favorite song. It was very cold and windy in Hendersonville that day but we all stood at attention at the cemetery when Mr. Ray Cash was given a 21-gun salute by members of the United States Army Honor Guard. After the service we returned to John's home for a light meal, then it was back home to New Jersey. Rest In Eternal Peace Mr. Ray Cash.

Ernie Anastos

I could not in good conscious write this book without mentioning my dear friend, Ernie Anastos and his connection to the Berkeley Carteret Hotel. If it were not for Ernie the hotel would have never been completed and Johnny Cash would never have been involved. I first met Ernie when he was the anchorman for WABC-TV News out of New York; presently Ernie anchors Fox News in New York City. Ernie, who is from the New England area, has adopted Asbury Park as his second hometown.

Richard Kennedy, Ernie Anastos, and Myself

Ernie joined the Army in the early '60s and was stationed at Fort Monmouth, New Jersey about a fifteen-minute drive from Asbury Park. Being a religious person, one Sunday he sought out a Greek Orthodox Church, which happened to be in Asbury Park. There he met and fell in love with a beautiful young lady named Kelly Coutros, who happened to be the pastor's daughter. Kelly went to Asbury Park High School and was in my Brother Sebastian's class. It was not until 1983 when Ernie and I were introduced by a mutual friend named George Michaels at a lunch meeting at Deal Golf and Country Club, another gentlemen at the meeting was Dick Levy, a VP with Cushman and Wakefield, the giant real estate firm in NYC and a friend of Ernie's. The meeting went great and we talked about Ernie getting involved in Asbury Park.

We soon developed a mutual respect for one another. My brother and I had recently purchased the abandoned landmark Berkeley Carteret Hotel and were looking to put together a group of investors to complete the costly renovations. Ernie jumped right in with both feet, and committed to an investment in the hotel around the same time as Johnny Cash did. Ernie really went out of his way to help; at that time, many local banks were leery about making an investment in Asbury Park mainly because of its history of bad government and the fact that it never fully recovered from race riots of the '60s. I had put together a group of investors and raised 3.6 million dollars in a matter of days, mostly from friends, including Ernie and Johnny Cash. We still had a problem in getting a bank to supply the needed first mortgage. Folks you will not see this very often and it shows a person's true character.

Soon after, Ernie came to town and spent the weekend at his in-laws house. On Saturday night we had a little fun as I took Ernie, who was not used to country music, to a little honky-tonk on Squankum Road in Howell, New Jersey, called Keifers Country Inn. To keep from being recognized, he wore old clothes and a baseball cap. This was a real joint: low ceilings, smoke-filled room's a hint of diesel fuel floating in the air, heffers dressed as cowgirls; you know what I mean a little on the heavy side, fighting over each other's boyfriend. This place was a real honky tonk something out of the old west, it had a small stage surrounded by a wooden fence and a bale of hay, that was elevated just a little above the dance floor yet the performers still had to duck their head to keep from hitting the ceiling. The air seemed stale and was not moving, after checking out the exhaust fan mounted on the window I soon discovered why. Simple answer the fan was running but the window was broken and closed so the same stale air was recirculating back inside. Around midnight we decided to have a nigh cap, I asked the waitress if they had Gran-Manier, she says "never heard of that but we do have Grand Dad." Despite their liquor selection Keifers did have great country music. Ernie had a blast, though the next day he told me that he had to throw away his jeans and shirt, as he could not get the smoky smell out of them.

Now after the fun on Saturday night we get to the real purpose of Ernie's visit. I had set up a meeting with Bill Robertson, the president of the First National Bank of Toms River NJ, some 20 miles south of Asbury Park for 11 o'clock on Monday morning. Ernie insisted on attending that meeting. We met at the Perkins Pancake House at the Asbury Traffic circle for breakfast where everyone recognized him, Ernie was viewed as the local boy who did good. After breakfast it's off to see Bill Robertson. We arrived on time for our meeting and were escorted into a conference room with several board members. Ernie's presence at that meeting and the fact that he committed not only to investing but to being a spokesman for the hotel was really all the board needed in formulating their decision to make the loan. On the spot, the bank committed to a four million five hundred thousand dollar first mortgage. The problem was we needed six million. However, the bank's legal lending limit for a single project was four and a half million. Ernie and Bill Robertson talked on how to get the additional funding. Ernie said that he knows some other bankers in New York City and would make a call to them. With that comment a light came on in Bill Robertson's head, He said Ernie you just gave me the answer, in front of us picks up the phone and soon Bill Robertson called Marine Midland Bank in Buffalo New York and over the phone got a commitment from them for the needed one million five hundred thousand dollars. All of that thanks to Ernie Anastos, who took the time to help me, not many people I know would take of their valuable time to do that, but Ernie did.

Finally with all our financing in place the reconstruction of the hotel is under way big time. The original hotel had 450 rooms, we completely gutted the building except for the magnificent banquet rooms on the second level, and they were restored to their former elegance of the '20's right down to making the plaster molds to recreate the ornamental ceilings. The original 450 rooms were smaller in size than today's standards so we reconstructed 256 rooms larger in size to meet today's market. Having said all of that, through his friend Dick Levy, Ernie helped me to find a joint venture partner to bid on the entire beachfront redevelopment project. Dick and Ernie introduced me to Donald Trump, and we actually had a meeting in his private office in Trump Tower. He said after our presentation that he was not interested, as he said his plate was full with projects in the New York area. Levy finally hooked me up with Joe Carabetta, a major New England developer, and we formed a partnership that eventually won the bid as the master redeveloper.

Ernie Anastos Emceeing The Johnny Cash Show
in Asbury Park 1985

On July 1, 1985, the hotel celebrated its 60th birthday with the lighting of the tower and fireworks; Ernie took time off to come down and lead that celebration. Timed with the grand opening of the hotel was the Johnny Cash concert on October 18. Ernie took the night off from the news, and drove down from New York just to attend and be the Master of Ceremonies. He and Johnny hit it off so much so that Ernie worked out an arrangement to interview Johnny and June for a new special show entitled families and actually spent the day with a film crew in their apartment.

Ernie was such a good friend that a year later when I was roasted as Man of the Year, he again took time off to drive to Asbury Park to emcee the roast. My one regret is that the hotel eventually went under and I let my good friends down, all of whom relied on me. But Ernie, thank you for being just plain you, a wonderful person to know and love.

The Bus Ride through Canada

This story starts at the United States Military Academy at West Point, New York. Johnny was performing a concert for the cadet corps, I had a driver bring me to West Point for the show as I planned to travel on the tour bus with John and June for the next few days heading for shows at two other venues before returning home by plane from Syracuse. Somewhere between a show date in Poughkeepsie and one in upstate New York, I was sitting in the forward seating area of the bus talking to Miss Kelly, the nurse who helped raised John Carter and continued to work for June both at home and on the road. It was just the two of us, for John was resting in his compartment and June in hers.

On this particular tour the band members traveled in a separate bus while the road crew traveled by car, as they had to stay behind to break down the show and load it into the trailer.

Depending on the length of the tour and the distance between venues, that would determine whether the band would travel in rented cars or on a leased second bus. Sometimes if everyone was staying in the same hotel the band would ride John's bus back and forth to the venue. Those guys in the road crew did not have an easy job; after loading up the show they had to drive to the next venue, get some sleep and then set up the entire show at a new location.

Anyway, Miss Kelly and I were talking when she told me a story about John. It seems that one day, while traveling between show dates in Canada, John asked Roger Morton, his bus driver, to pull over and stop at the next convenience store that he could find. Roger soon pulled over and John got off the bus and went into this store to get a snack. He was recognized by a woman who walked up to

103

him and told Johnny that she and her husband were big fans, and could she please get an autographed photo for her husband who was very ill and confined to a bed. Johnny asked Roger to go on the bus and get a photo, which John promptly signed.

This woman could not thank him enough then said that she only lived down the road about a mile and was there any way that that Johnny could stop and see her husband as he was terminally ill, and it would mean so much to him. Johnny apologized and said "Ma'am I am sorry, but I don't have time, as I must get to the next city to do a show." The woman said she understood, and John boarded the bus and headed to his next stop.

According to Miss Kelly after John got on the bus they headed to the next venue when he sat down and told her the story of the lady he had just met and the sorrowful look she had on her face as he was walking out of the store. After thinking about it for a few minutes and looking at his watch, he told Roger to turn the bus around and head back to the store. He was hoping the lady was still there. She was, and John then escorted her on the bus as she directed Roger to her house. True to his convictions, Johnny went into her home and comforted her husband, posed for a couple of photos and gave him a Bible that he had on the bus. Johnny then apologized for having to leave, got back on the bus and went on his way.

Folks, this story must be true as Miss Kelly told me so.

Johnny always stopping to say Hello to his admirers
Here he is in Bimini with the locals

June Carter Cash: Restorative

In 1987, June Carter Cash wrote a book called *From the Heart.* It was a series of vignettes about people that she had befriended and who had made an impact on her life, from the likes of Hank Williams to Elvis Presley to yours truly. I am truly honored and blessed that she dedicated a chapter to me.

RESTORATIVE

There's no way to explain how Johnny Cash and June Carter Cash got involved in restoring downtown Asbury Park, New Jersey. When I try to explain it, nothing makes sense. It has something to do with giving back some glory to a place that deserves it, but you really have to be there to understand.

115

"There's no way to explain how Johnny Cash and June Carter Cash got involved in restoring downtown   Asbury Park, New Jersey. When I try to explain it, nothing makes sense. It has something to do with giving back some glory to a place that deserves it, but you really have to be there to understand." These words written by June Carter Cash are contained in the introduction of chapter thirty that she simply called "Restorative"

There, June went into detail on how she first met me as I used to bring Kramer guitars and basses to their show for Bob Wootton and Marshall Grant. For the longest time, June thought of me as a man that made guitars by hand in my garage one at a time. She was shocked when Bob told her that the guitars were made in a factory and that I owned the factory. It took her several years before she learned that my main business was construction and development, and the guitar business was a sideline.

One of the interesting tidbits in the story was when Hurricane Gloria came barreling down the east coast in July of 1985, packing winds over 100 miles per hour headed right for Asbury Park and the almost completed Berkeley Carteret Hotel. On the day of the storm my construction company still had over 40 men working on the interior finishes and exterior landscaping. To protect the large windows on the first floor east side, I instructed my foreman to block the windows by parking a large tractor trailer parallel to them, thus stopping any wind gust from a direct hit. This worked perfectly as no windows were shattered; we also installed plywood over the glass doors.

We did have one serious problem, though: the architect specified a state-of-the-art Carlisle Rubber Roof to be applied over all the high roof areas. This design was much like a swimming pool liner except it was made of heavy rubber vulcanized together to form a solid sheet to the exact size and shape of the roof. For example, if the roof was 60 feet wide and you had parapet walls 3 feet high on each side, the rubber would be 66 feet wide and seamless, to allow the rubber to go up the parapct, right to the copping, thus making the entire roof one waterproof piece.

One problem with this type of roof is you cannot penetrate the rubber with nails to hold it down, as that could cause leaks. The roof was instead held down with ballast in the form of smooth surface river gravel. This not only held down the roof but acted to protect the roof from the ultraviolet light from the sun, plus the gravel would break up any suction that could be caused by strong winds passing over and causing what is known as uplift.

This looked like the perfect roof, but it had its pitfalls. The hotel roof was penetrated by vent stacks and large exhaust fans mounted on wooden curbs, which were flashed to the roof. The hotel was basically built in the shape of a large X, and at the end of each wing we constructed an exit stair tower to meet the new code requirements; directly above each stair tower was a large exhaust fan.

On the morning in question, the storm hit around 9 a.m., with wind gusts over 125 miles per hour, though only light rain. I had one of our security people walk the hotel and look for any signs of trouble. All of a sudden, he came running down to me on the first floor with a report that stones were pouring down the southeast stair tower. I started climbing the stairs and heard stones dropping all over the place.

By the time I got to the eighth floor right outside of Johnny's apartment, I was out of breath and needed a break. But I couldn't take one, as I saw the problem: the wind had come across the roof with such force that it ripped the exhaust fan right off the roof, leaving a four-foot by four-foot hole that I could look right through to see daylight. I caught my breath and ran down the other end of the hall to a stair going directly to the roof and up I went, I was shocked at what I saw next the rubber roof was literally blowing off. If you saw the rubber it had stretched and looked just like a giant beach ball, about 30 feet in diameter and was flapping around. As the wind would subside momentarily the rubber would then lie down, when another gust would come by up it went again.

I later found out from an expert what caused the problem. When strong winds pass over a smooth surface a vacuum is created and in this case the winds of 125mph sucked up the rubber roof .This would not have occurred if the stones stayed in place and didn't blow off dropping

106

through the opening left by the exhaust fan. The stones besides acting as ballast also break up the suction preventing the uplift. Having said all that, I will now quote from June's book.

"Hey, John, look here at this newspaper. Is that Henry? Yeah, the one in the middle is Henry .The one sitting on that big balloon with those six other men clinging to the edge of it.It looks as if it is blowing away" . "Let me see. It's not a balloon, June. It's the roof of the Berkeley Carteret Hotel in Asbury Park, New Jersey. Can you believe that seven men have got the nerve to hold down and ride on a rubber roof that is brand new and literally being raised by a hurricane?" Hold her, Henry. Don't let her go. Hang on to that roof. We need it"……………

June had just seen a cover story in the local paper that featured a photo of me and several of my men lying on that rubber roof to hold it down and keep it from blowing entirely off. What saved the day was that my crew was still on the job and I had them use the passenger elevator and raise up about 500 concrete block weighing 80 pounds each ,and walk them to the roof level. We then replaced the weight of each man lying prone with concrete blocks. Believe it or not it worked. It might not meet OSHA standards but it did the job.

Back to Junes book "Within the dream of a good friend, a contractor, builder, I play the part of happiness and hope, as I grow older, I'll be able to preserve me, a person and think back to the splendor of my youth" "I figured Henry was serious when he refused to blow away in that hurricane" Thank you June Carter Cash for your beautiful and thoughtful words of wisdom. I will always cherish our friendship.

Photos Courtesy of Dave Gamble

107

Brother Sebastian

The youngest member of our family of two boys and two girls is my brother Sebastian, Sam for short; although as a kid we just called him Brother. I am the oldest, and there is a six year difference between us. As kids growing up, we had the best of times, and were best of friends; we even shared a bedroom together. When Sam graduated from college he came to work in my company, The Henry V. Vaccaro Corp, and was an integral part of our success. Sam was the CFO and had complete charge of the accounting and computer department. In the eighties we became equal partners in the Berkeley Carteret Hotel and all our joint real estate holdings in Asbury Park, We were also equal partners in a limited partnership entity called Carabetta Vaccaro Developers, LLC that owned the rights to the billion-dollar redevelopment project along the Asbury Park beachfront.

As brothers, from time to time, we did disagree. As I was the older brother, I thought that I was the boss even though we were partners. I never really gave Sam all the credit that he deserved for the success of our various business ventures. I regret that today, and know I never would have been as successful as I was without my brother guarding my back. In retrospect, I should not have been so stubborn and should have listened to him more than I did.

In 1992, almost 33 years to the day of my father's heart attack and death, Sam was rushed to Jersey Shore Medical Center with a massive heart attack. It was so severe that the doctors performed emergency quadruple bypass surgery, and thank God it was successful. Sam was not quite out of the woods yet, as his heart had suffered permanent damage and he had to be flown by helicopter to Lankenau Medical Center, located on the main line near Philadelphia, Pennsylvania. Sam became only the second recipient in the United States to have a defibrillator implanted in his side and wired directly to his heart. Things seemed to be going well for a time, then it was discovered that the defibrillator had a flaw and was recalled, meaning more surgery to install a new one. That went well until an infection developed that was potentially life-threatening, and then it was back to Lankenau for further treatment.

On Friday night, December 18, 1992, Johnny Cash was performing at the State Theater in Easton Pennsylvania. While backstage before the show John had asked about my brother, and I told him that Sam was back in Lankenau Hospital in Ardmore, near Philadelphia. John replied, "Can we see him tomorrow morning?"

I was astonished, John said, give Jack Shaw the directions, we will all go to the hospital to visit Sam; it is not that far out of our way as we are heading south toward Washington DC. I contacted the bus driver, I don't recall his name as Roger Morton the regular driver had left the Johnny Cash Show at this point, and arranged to meet the bus at the Conshohocken Exit of the Pennsylvania Turnpike, at 10 a.m. the next day, right on time, Johnny's driver pulled off the Turnpike and I led the way in my car to the hospital. John's bus drove up to the front door of the hospital and out came Johnny, June, John Carter and Jack Shaw. Jack, who is also a friend of mine, is a steeplejack by profession and an ordained minister, who was traveling with Johnny on some of his tours; Jack was also one heck of a guitar player and would occasionally play rhythm guitar on the shows. Johnny sometimes would have him travel on tour for a little spiritual uplifting, as he would introduce Jack to the audience as a minister that was available to speak to anyone that needed his counseling during the intermission, or after the show.

All heads turned as Johnny and his entourage entered the hospital. After getting directions to my brother's room, they proceeded into the elevator and exited on the fourth floor and headed right for his room. (I had not told Sam in advance that Johnny was going to pay him a visit.) When Johnny Cash went into Sam's room you could have heard a pin drop. A huge smile came over Sam's face when they entered his room, and everyone gathered around as Jack Shaw read a prayer from the Bible and Johnny, June and John Carter all said private prayers. All in all, they spent over a half-hour with Sam. That visit lifted up his spirits so much that three days, later Sam came home.

It ain't over yet, although Sam came home, over the next couple of years his heart continued to weaken, so in February of 1996 Sam was back in the hospital, this time at the University of Pennsylvania Medical Center awaiting a heart transplant. Thanks to the Good Lord, on June 13, 1996, a new heart was flown in by helicopter. And at 4 a.m. Sam's chest was opened and a new gift of life was transplanted into my brother.

A week later, I was traveling with John on the bus returning from Washington DC on its way to New York City, when John picked up the mobile phone and called my brother. He told him how happy he was for him and that he was sending Sam a gift. That gift was a boxed set of cassettes tapes of Johnny Cash reading the entire New Testament of the Bible. Thank you, Dear Lord, for my brother Sebastian is still here sixteen years later. And thank you, Johnny Cash for inspiring him to get well.

JOHNNY'S SPECIAL FRIEND ,NICKY PAOLANTONIO
aka "Hot Spot DJ Nicky"

Johnny Cash had this way and demeanor about him that seemed to attract people from all walks of life, young and old, rich or poor alike. A case in point, during my high school days I had a classmate named Vito Paolantonio, whose younger brother Nick married my neighbor Ann Strano. Ann had two older brothers Harry and Bob we were all close friends. Well over the years we kind of drifted apart until one day, out of the clear blue sky, Bob Strano called me on the phone and said that his nephew Nicky, Nick and Ann's son was a big Johnny Cash fan and he would to love to see Johnny in concert someday.

Bob proceeded to tell me that Nicky who is a special needs child was a huge fan of Johnny Cash after first seeing him on the Muppet Show and then on Sesame Street .Nicky had his father go out and buy every Johnny Cash album he could find, which Nicky listened to day and night, after all Nicky wanted everyone to know that he loved "The Man in Black"

Bob found out that Johnny and June were performing at The Trump Casino in Atlantic City and was there any way I could get tickets for Nicky and his mom has he has never been to a live concert. Absolutely, I called Lou Robin Johnny's manager and sure enough he arranged to get me extra tickets for the show including backstage passes for Nicky and his mom.
I had called June earlier in the day and told her about Nicky, she said to please bring him back stage about a half hour before the show so John could spend some time with him.

I met Ann and Nicky in the lobby of the casino and quickly escorted them back to John's dressing room. Johnny invited them in and introduced Nicky to everybody from John Carter,June to Helen and Anita as well as Bob Wootton,Fluke and Earl Poole Ball. Johnny started talking to Nicky who was about fourteen years old at the time. Nicky shook his hand and Johnny said I understand that you have seen me on television,and do you have a favorite song. Nicky said yes but I don't remember the name of the song, but it has something to do with a fire. Johnny,do you think it could be "Ring of Fire" Nicky jumped up and said excitedly "that's it"

Johnny told Nicky when you're in the audience watching the show how about I sing that song for you, Nicky was so excited,Johnny then said come back here after the show and tell me if you like it. I escorted them to the auditorium and to their seats and told Ann after the show to meet me at the side door and we would all go back and say goodbye to Johnny and June.

True to his word Johnny from the stage said "I have a special dedication tonight to my new friend Nicky , Nicky this one is for you ,as Johnny then continued to sing 'Ring of Fire. After the concert we met at the side door and back to John's dressing room where he asked Nicky if he enjoyed the show, Nicky put both of his arms around Johnny and hugged him Johnny hugged him back and as a parting gesture to his new found friend Johnny gave Nicky one of the harmonicas he used in singing "Orange Blossom Special " as well as a lifetime all access backstage pass which allowed Nicky to visit Johnny at any show Nicky attended. Those are Nicky's most prized possessions.

Johnny was such an inspiration to Nicky that he took voice lessons for years and became an accomplished singer, Nicky graduated from high school and lost 100 pounds, started his own DJ business called "Hot Spot DJ Nicky" and whenever he has a gig, Nicky dedicates the song "Ring of Fire" to his friend for life Johnny Cash

Chapter 16
You Aint No Johnny Cash

©www.DebraRothenberg.com

The Jon Bon Jovi I Used to know

The purpose of this story is to draw a comparison between two artists both superstars and how they handled fame. According to his commercial for Advil, Jon Bon Jovi is a singer, songwriter, philanthropist and father. Jon is all of those things but he kind of forgot one thing that makes a man a real man: its one simple word called humility.

I first met Jon in 1986 at the Kramer Guitar Factory, where I was a principal stockholder and Chairman of the Board. The guitar company at that juncture was making instruments for just about every heavy metal band in the country, thanks to our major endorsement from Eddie Van Halen. Both Jon Bon Jovi and his sidekick Richie Sambora were Kramer endorsees. At that time in my life I was 45 years old, full of piss and vinegar, and on top of the world.

During the '80s, I was heralded as a local hero for trying to restore my hometown of Asbury Park—the town that my father loved, and the people he died for. Asbury Park had gone through some rough times; the riots of the late '60s which left part of the city in shambles. My goal was to use everything in my power to bring the city back to its former glory, as my family was deeply rooted there. In addition to my hard-working and humanitarian father, my grandfather, Henry A. Vaccaro, was responsible for the effort to change city's form of government in 1938. My aunt Mary Martin was the city clerk for over 30 years; my uncle, Dr. Henry J. Vaccaro, M.D., was the first Independent elected to the city council; and finally my daughter, Toni Vaccaro, was the youngest female in the state to be elected to a city council post.

I think that my stock in town really started to rise in 1982, when it was publicly announced that my brother and I had purchased the boarded up Berkeley Carteret Hotel on the beachfront and planned on restoring it. Then with the announcement of Johnny Cash's involvement in not only the hotel but in the redevelopment project as well, it became front-page news all over the country. The hotel had been closed for eight years when my brother and I purchased it.

The Berkeley Carteret Hotel was constructed in 1927 and was the cornerstone of the once magnificent Asbury Park beachfront, situated directly across the street from the Atlantic Ocean. The hotel has a long history with my family, my grandfather planted the grass there as a gardener in 1927, my mother and father were married there in 1939, my dad was knighted by a representative of Pope John XXIII there in 1959 and I was married to Diane there in 1960.

During WWII, it was taken over by the British Navy and became the only piece of real estate in the world ever named as a ship: the *HMS Asbury*. We started restoring the hotel in 1983 at a cost of 15 million dollars, with a grand reopening scheduled the following year. The project won an award from HUD in Washington D.C. as the best project in the United States using private and public funds. Along with the hotel, I was a major partner in the oceanfront redevelopment project and so my name was always front-page news in the local papers, the *Asbury Park Press*, the *Coaster*, and several New Jersey magazines. The local YMCA, and the Asbury Park Chamber of Commerce both named me Man of the Year, and bumper stickers were even printed with sayings like "Asbury Park (loves) Henry Vaccaro," and "How does Asbury Park spell relief? V-A-C-C-A-R-O." So with all that hype, publicity, and notoriety going on, Jon Bon Jovi appeared from out of nowhere and wanted to meet me. This occurred in the summer of 1986, at the Kramer Guitar Factory in Neptune, New Jersey.

To be honest I didn't know much about Bon Jovi or his music at that time, as I was more into country music. Jon picked me up in his jeep and asked me to guide him around Asbury Park and explain the redevelopment project. As he drove the short two miles to Asbury Park, I directed him through the downtown business area to the beachfront. We started our little tour at the southern end of the beach near the Casino and Carousel House and drove north about a mile to Deal Lake. We then turned around and headed back to the hotel for lunch. Jon was very pleasant and I do believe at this first meeting that we enjoyed each other's company and hit it off. He asked me a lot of questions about Johnny Cash: how I'd met him, how long I had known him, about our fishing trips, and how often did Johnny come to Asbury Park. In fact young Jon Bon Jovi seemed a little star-struck when talking about Johnny Cash.

In March of 1987, Jon called and left a message with my secretary saying he wanted to invite me and my son to his concert on April 2ⁿᵈ at the Spectrum in Philadelphia. At first I didn't return the call as I had an awful lot going on, but Jon persisted and called a second time. He said he really wanted both of us to attend, and that tickets and backstage passes would be waiting at the box office.

The Spectrum was about a two hour drive from Asbury Park, and when Henry Jr. and I arrived; sure enough there were two front row tickets and backstage passes at the will-call window of the box office. The seats were great, the show was great. Jon Bon Jovi was fantastic even though his music was a little loud for my middle-aged hearing.

After the show, we showed our backstage passes to the security guard who promptly escorted us to the dress-

Backstage at a Bon Jovi Show: The Great Les Paul, Richie Sambora and Me

ing room. I knocked on the door, which was opened by Jon's girlfriend Dorothea, and we were let in and cordially welcomed by Jon, who was now wearing a silk robe, much like the type a prizefighter would wear. He apologized for being "all sweaty," hugged me, and asked what we thought of the show. I responded that it was great, and Henry Jr. also congratulated him as well.

But I was mystified at Jon's next statement: "Henry, your not going to believe this but while I was on stage I saw you in the audience and was thinking of you. I was wondering how you think I compare to Johnny Cash." I replied, "Your show was fabulous but his music is completely different than yours, and his show is different, but again you were great." He thanked me. After some small talk and refreshments we left to drive home, and on the way, Henry Jr. said "Dad, I can't believe Jon Bon Jovi made such a big deal out of you, like *you're* the rock star!"

114

Fast forward to December 9, 1987. The Berkeley Carteret Hotel is hosting a Gala Event, the world premiere of Danny DeVito's movie *Throw Momma from the Train*. Danny DeVito, also a native of Asbury Park, thought it fitting enough to unveil his new movie, which he'd directed in his hometown. The before- and after-parties were hosted in the hotel's Crystal Ballroom while the actual premiere of the film was held across the street at the Paramount Theater. Celebrities like New Jersey Governor Tom Kean, Christopher Reeve, Danny DeVito, Anne Ramsey, Carol Kane, James L. Brooks, Jon Bon Jovi, Richie Sambora, Tico Torres, David Bryan, and Celeste Holm walked the red carpet from the hotel to the theater, spotlights beaming into the sky.

(Debra L. Rothenberg)
Jon and long-time love, Dorothea Hurley, celebrate the premier of "Throw Mama From The Train" at the Berkeley Carteret Hotel in Asbury Park, N.J.

Jon stayed locally in the area; sometimes I would bump into him and Dorothea at a restaurant in Bradley Beach called Jakes. I didn't see much of him in 1988, as the band seemed to always be on tour. During the spring of 1989, most of the band members stayed at the Berkeley including Doc McGhee, the band's manager. Jon stayed with Dorothea in a very small motel suite at 100 Second Avenue near the ocean in Bradley Beach, and the Berkeley Carteret was used as the east coast base for that leg of the Bon Jovi Tour. A chartered jet was now stationed at Wall Airport; a few miles away, allowing the band to fly to their venues in the five state areas, return to airport and then come to Asbury Park at night.

(Debra L. Rothenberg)
Later, they are joined by the film's director and co-star, Danny DeVito (standing) and Asbury Park developer, Henry Vaccaro (far right).

It was on one of these dates that I was kidnapped by Richie Sambora, forced into a van and taken to Wall Airport, then pushed onto a plane where I accompanied the entire band consisting of Jon Bon Jovi, Richie Sambora, Tico Torres, David Bryan Alec John Such and their girlfriends to Syracuse and on to the Carrier Dome for their concert.

Well, okay, I was not exactly *kidnapped*. It just so happened that I was at the Berkeley Carteret around 4 pm on March 3 1989 when Ritchie Sambora appeared in the lobby and asked me what I was doing. Not much, come with us, where are you going? To Syracuse for a show. So off to Syracuse I went on the Bon Jovi Jet. At the concert, I had the best seat in the house on stage just to the left of Richie and his many Kramer guitars. In fact, I almost went flying when the pyrotechnics went off right next to me; that's how close I was to the action. During the show I remember a harness being put around Jon as he was lifted up about 80 to 90 feet into the air to make it appear that he was flying out over the audience while he sang. After the show, it was back to the airport in a van and then our flight home. After arriving at the airport, Jon realized that he'd left his silk robe in the dressing room. This was 1989, pre-cell phone, so guess what? We turned around and headed back to the Carrier Dome for his robe, then back to airport again for the flight home.

A few days later, I saw Jon and he asked a favor of me. Could I possibly look after Dorothea as he would be away on tour for the next 5 days.
He wanted to make sure that she would be safe. Could I maybe take her out to dinner and he would reimburse me I agreed. So two days later on a Saturday night Dorothea and I went out to the Cypress Inn located in Wanamassa, then to a small Country Music Club called Kiefer's

Richie Sambora
A Musician Behind His Guitar

Featured in this photo is Richie's personally designed Kramer guitar which he used on the Bon Jovi 'Slippery When Wet' tour. This guitar is now available to you through Kramer Music Products with special features including: star shaped pearl inlays, Seymour Duncan™ pickups and the 'Original Floyd Rose Tremolo'.

For Further Details Visit Your Nearest Kramer Dealer

KRAMER

hvinthehouse

Country Inn, on Squankum Road in nearby Howell, New Jersey, and we finally ended up at the Stone Pony in Asbury Park. I then took her back to the motel in Bradley Beach, where we parted company. Several days later after returning home, Jon called to thank me. A month later he and Dorothea flew to Las Vegas on a whim and got married.

I lived in Interlaken back then, in a magnificent estate that once belonged to my parents. It sat on an acre of land overlooking the lake, with a large yard and 20x40 swimming pool. Another time, while Jon was on tour, Dorothea and a girlfriend stopped by and spent part of the afternoon around the pool.

The next thing of significance is a phone call from Doc Mc Ghee, Bon Jovi 's manager. Is it possible for you to meet me with me and our accountant for lunch tomorrow at the hotel. I had no idea what the meeting was about, but for a free lunch why not. When we sat down Doc introduced me to a gentleman by the name of Bruce Kolbrenner CPA the accountant for the Bon Jovi organization.

Doc said that "Jon has a lot of respect for you", that's why I invited you for lunch. Bruce then went on to say that the boys are going on a sold out world tour, and they should all make lots of money. When they get home they all want to buy new houses, and could I recommend a good lawyer that is honest and fair, I did not hesitate and highly recommend Dick Mc Omber who not only was my corporate attorney and personal attorney but trusted friend. Well low and behold Richard McOmber Esq. from Red Bank NJ based upon my recommendation is hired to represent Jon and all the other band members, not only for the purchase of their homes but for other non-related entertainment matters as well.

Kramer Guitar Company in the late '80s was a major force in the music industry, having been named by Guitar Player Magazine in 1988 as the best-selling guitar in the country. Kramer started to branch out into other entertainment venues, and in fact, put together the Moscow Music Peace Festival in Russia. This was the first major heavy metal music event ever to be held in Russia. This came about after Kramer started to manage a Russian band named Gorky Park, and then Dennis Berardi the president of Kramer got this brainstorm to become a concert promoter. As a result, Dennis put together all the major bands that endorsed Kramer, and the next thing you knew, the Peace Festival was set for two days in August of 1989 at Lenin Stadium. The bands included Bon Jovi, Motley Crue, Ozzy Osbourne, Skid Row, Cinderella and The Scorpions.

Throughout the '90s, Bon Jovi was always on tour so I saw very little of Jon. He and Dorothea now married moved into a new home at 22 Somerset Drive in Rumson, New Jerssey and my friend Dick McOmber handled the closing. When I found out about it I sent a housewarming present to them. Jon personally called to thank me and invited me over for dinner. The house was beautiful, with a small studio in the lower

VP of manufacturing Andy Papiccio, Me, June, Johnny and VP of Sales Tony Costello outside the Kramer Factory

level. I mentioned to him that we were planning to put some celebrity memorabilia on display at the hotel, so he then gave me a pair of green sequined pants that he'd worn on tour, which he then autographed.

In July of 1990, Jon called to ask if he could hold a news conference for the foreign press in Johnny Cash's suite at the Berkeley Carteret Hotel. I replied that I would call Johnny and ask his permission, which he graciously granted. So we hosted a two-day media event for Jon Bon Jovi timed with the release of his new solo project "Blaze of Glory" from the *Young Guns* movie soundtrack.

Around this time period I was starting to get a lot of negative press, as the billion-dollar redevelopment project was starting to go sour and without that project, the hotel was having a tough time. One phase of the project called for the restoration of the Convention Hall and Paramount Theater, which stood literally 200 feet from the hotel. That restoration never happened, and without the Convention Hall in full operation especially in the winter months, the hotel could not survive. It was now front-page news that the hotel was also in financial trouble and as the

Henry Jr. Escorting Jon to Johnny Cash's Penthouse for "Young Guns" Interviews

hometown hero, I took the fall. The hotel eventually filed for bankruptcy. This was front page news and it sold newspapers.

The reason that I bring these things up, is that all of a sudden my relationship with Jon Bon Jovi evaporated very quickly. One night I saw him along with an entourage go into Jake's restaurant in Bradley Beach for dinner. I was sitting with a friend at a corner table and he walked right by, as if I were invisible. I did not say anything and will give him the benefit of the doubt; maybe he didn't see me as he was preoccupied. After his party sat down in the next room I called the waitress over and told her to send a bottle of wine over to Mr. Bon Jovi's table, she said. "Who should I say it's from." "Tell him it's from someone he used to know," I said, then quickly paid my check and walked out.

As I stated earlier Jon and Dorothea on a whim went to Las Vegas and secretly got married. A year or so later they held a lavish wedding reception at the South Street Seaport in New York City. Guess who got invited to the reception, not me. But my lawyer Dick McOmber and his wife, Adrian. The McOmber's office walls are now graced with several Gold and Platinum Bon Jovi albums all dedicated to them.

In the early 2000s, Bon Jovi performed a concert in Convention Hall in Asbury Park, I believe it was for some charity, I received two tickets from Richie Sambora and went backstage into their dressing room before the show, where I spent some time with Tico, David and Richie. They introduced me to their new bass player, Hugh McDonald, who had taken over for Alec John several years earlier; that's how long it had been since I'd seen the guy's. Jon had a separate dressing room on the opposite side of the stage and was not available prior to the show. I did see his father who was standing alone on the convention floor area he told me that Jon needs to meditate before performing. After the show I yelled to Jon who was on the way to his dressing room he turned around and then kept on walking, maybe he just didn't see me. But that's ok.

The last time I saw Jon Bon Jovi was after he did a set at the Stone Pony in Asbury Park for the benefit of 9-11 victims. He was sitting at the bar speaking with someone, and when they finished I walked up to him. I said "Hey, Jon," he turned and said, "Henry, right?" Yeah it's Henry.

Well, after a little small talk about the submarine movie he was in, I just could not resist any longer. I had to tell him how I felt. I looked straight at him and his fluffy hair and said, "You know something, Jon? You ain't no Johnny Cash." He looked bewildered, as I turned and walked out, I have not seen or heard from him since.

Chapter 17
New Years in Jamaica
1993 -1994

I love to tell this story as a backdrop to my friendship with Johnny and my life in the '80s and to show the contrast of how an Icon like Johnny Cash stays true to his friendships where as a flighty Bon Jovi is only loyal to his fame.

In 1982, when my brother and I purchased the hotel, we put together a little private investment group that included among others Johnny Cash, June Carter Cash, and Ernie Anastos. After a fifteen-million dollar restoration it reopened in 1986. Johnny and June had the eighth floor penthouse apartment facing southeast; it was furnished with many of their antiques brought from Nashville. Things went well for the next five years, and then the bottom fell out of the economy, the bank that held the mortgage failed, and we also lost our major corporate clients. We were up shit's creek, literally, when raw sewage washed up on the beach over one 4th of July weekend and ruined the entire summer season, not only that year but the next. Eventually the hotel failed, forcing us to file for bankruptcy.

The hotel was auctioned off and sold, and I then also filed for personal bankruptcy as well. Folks, here is where you separate the men from the boys. If you ever go bankrupt or get divorced, that's when you find out who your true friends are, people who you thought were your friends have a mysterious way of disappearing.

Now for the meat of the story on December 12, 1993, I was at my girlfriend's house, when out of the clear blue sky her phone rang and on the other end it's Johnny Cash. To this day I don't know how he got her phone number, but it doesn't matter. She handed the phone to me, and I heard, "Henry, it's John. How are you doing? June and I are worried about you, are you ok?"

119

"Yes," I replied, still startled.

"Are you sure?" he asked again. "What are you doing for the holidays?"

"I'm just staying home," I told him.

"No, that's not fair you're coming to Jamaica with us and to make sure that you show up I'm sending you the plane fare tomorrow. You're going to spend the holidays with our family, at Cinnamon Hill in Jamaica."

The very next day Johnny 's sister Reba who ran Johnny's office named The House of Cash called my office and wanted to know what airport I wanted to fly from, and the day after that a Federal Express package arrived with my round trip ticket. I landed at Montego Bay airport on December 26th, 1993. This was my first trip to Jamaica, and after getting my luggage, I cleared customs. But then I started to feel a little uneasy, as there was no one waiting to meet me.

Well, what the hell do I do? I didn't have Johnny's address or phone number and I'm stranded, so I walked out of the airport looking for a cab driver that could get me to Johnny's home. The only thing that I knew was that it was called Cinnamon Hill, located near a Great House named Rose Hall. I finally found a cab driver who seemed to know where Johnny lived. After getting into his car I had this uneasy feeling like I was taking my life into my own hands. This guy drove an ancient car all over the highway, which ran parallel to the Caribbean Sea. After what seemed like an hour but was less than thirty minutes, he finally turned off the main thoroughfare onto a dirt road heading up a hill away from the ocean. The next thing I see are two black men, one with a rifle another with a machine gun, I'm scared to death.

The guy with the machine gun approached the car. I was cowering in the back seat when he said "Welcome to Cinnamon Hill!" I almost fainted. I just pictured all this voodoo crap that you hear about in Jamaica, and I'm this token white dude surrounded by three natives.

Pulling into Cinnamon Hill

John Carter at the Gates

One of the guards escorted me through the main gate into a courtyard where I was met by the housekeeper, who said Mr. and Mrs. Cash were in town and would be back later. She showed me to beautifully appointed bedroom where I deposited my luggage. I soon learned that Billy Graham had stayed in that very room the year before and so June had renamed it "The Billy Graham Room." The bed that I was going to be sleeping in hence was known as "The Billy Graham Bed," and it was a Jamaican antique four-poster bed made of native dark wood with a beautiful hand-carved headboard that seemed wider than normal. Paul McCartney stayed in this room the year before Billy.

I had no sooner unpacked when John Carter came in and greeted me. We went down to the pool and he told me about the armed security, reminding me that about twelve years earlier they were robbed at gunpoint while having dinner and Johnny was not taking any more chances. Johnny Cash was a popular figure in Jamaica, as he did benefit concerts for the locals, and would

even ship down food and clothing to them. Just his presence in Jamaica and the fact that he had a home there helped the image of the island. As the story goes, the robbery suspects were quickly apprehended by the police, then native justice soon prevailed and somehow mysteriously they were both killed trying to escape. You get the point. That's Jamaican justice.

Soon Johnny and June arrived and welcomed me like I was the missing part of their family, explaining that they'd thought I was getting in the *next* day, but were very happy to see me now. You can't imagine how good they made me feel, as I was still depressed from my bankruptcy. Here I was, a small town guy from New Jersey broke as a skunk, spending the holidays and New Year's with my idol, the biggest country artist of all time, and his family at their magnificent hideaway in paradise. I was so grateful.

121

Tiffany Lowe Johnny and Junes Granddaughter

One by one other family members came in, including Johnny's daughter Cindy and her daughter and Carlene Carter's daughter Tiffany Lowe, their granddaughter. I had met both Cindy and Tiffany years before at the Hendersonville, Tennessee house and also at various times on the road. Later that day four other house guests arrived from California.

They were none other than Rick Rubin, Johnny's new record producer, with his lady friend, and Anthony Kiedis of the Red Hot Chili Peppers and his model girlfriend. I knew who Rick Rubin was, but I can honestly say I'd never heard of Anthony Kiedis, although I did hear of the Red Hot Chili Peppers as they once played in Asbury Park.

Anthony, June and anthony's Friend

Rick Rubin Me and Rick's guest

The Cinnamon Hill home was built like a fort to withstand any hurricane. One corner of the house, which stood about two stories tall, was shaped like the bow of a ship and pointed in the direction of the prevailing winds, toward the sea. If a hurricane came, it would break up the force of the wind so as not to hit the house broadside, and it worked. After visiting Cinnamon Hill it was not hard to understand why John and June loved it so much. It sits on top of this gently sloping hill surrounded on three sides by a golf course and overlooks the Caribbean Sea.

122

Around six o'clock we all sat down in the formal dining room that had a table large enough for all twelve of us. After sitting down, we all held hands as Johnny said a prayer before our meal. There were fresh flowers on the table and fresh fruit to eat—mango, papaya, oranges, etc. The main course was steak with fresh vegetables and homemade pastry for dessert.

During the time I stayed there, some nights after dinner we would all sit around the living room as Johnny played and sang for all of us. I still can't believe it: my own private concert.

John at the Head of the Table

Pickin' Time

On the third day we all went by motorized golf carts down to one of the nearby beach resorts for lunch, a magnificent setting right on the water. I was shocked at all these giggling girls that recognized not Johnny but Anthony Kiedis—well, so much for the younger generation. On another day, John Carter and his girlfriend, Anthony and his model, and Tiffany and I took a trip to the resort town of Negril, about a two hour drive. I really got to know Anthony on this ride; he is quite a guy, far from that rock and roll persona. He told me about a trip he took to the jungles of New Guinea where he got lost and didn't think he would survive. The first night, he said,

John carter, anthony and Myself on our hike around the Island

while lying in a sleeping bag, some type of insect crawled inside his ear and laid eggs. It got infected several days later and his buddy had to pull it out with tweezers. Never again, he said. I could relate to that experience having traveled to the jungles of Guadalcanal in the Solomon Islands on one of my WWII adventures and saw first-hand what our Marines went through.

We decided to stop for lunch at one of the resorts and go for a swim. All the brave ones put on harnesses and went flying on kites that were pulled behind a speedboat, while I watched. We then drove back to Cinnamon Hill. The next day we all hung around the house went swimming in the pool and took a very leisurely long walk around the golf course, all the way to the Caribbean Sea and back.

New Year's Eve was special, too. After an early dinner we were all invited to John Rollins' private beach to welcome in the New Year; Mr. Rollins was the largest private landowner in Jamaica, and a longtime friend of Johnny and June. Cinnamon Hill had in fact been purchased from John Rollins. When it was time to leave for the beach, John grabbed his guitar case, and then he and I got in his car for a very scary drive down an unlit dirt road heading to the beach. When we finally arrived, I was amazed to see a tremendous pile of large bamboo trees, about five or six inches in diameter, standing upright and bunched together, almost like the shape of a giant teepee. This was to become our bonfire.

Around 11 o'clock, June, John Carter and the other guests had just arrived, along with John and Michele Rollins, their family and their guests, totaling over a hundred, including the Prime Minister of Jamaica. Just picture this scene: you're sitting on a beach chair on a private beach beside Johnny Cash and John Rollins. A large bonfire is lit directly in front of you, then Johnny pulls out his guitar from its case, stretches out his long legs and starts picking and singing. The fire by this time is forty or fifty feet in the air, almost like a volcano ready to erupt and everyone is singing along with Johnny. Truly paradise.

John Rollins. Johnny and I sitting at the bon fire on the beach at the Rollins Estate

After eight or ten songs, John Rollins turned to Johnny and said, "Let's sing some old songs that we used to sing in church." Johnny would strum a note and do the intro to the song, and then we'd all chime in and eventually sang every gospel song that he could remember, from "Onward Christian Soldiers" to "The Old Rugged Cross." We stayed past midnight singing, eating and drinking tropical Jamaican fare before heading home.

New Year's Day, too, was special in Jamaica, as I came to find out. It was a tradition at Mr. Rollins' estate, as both the Cash and Rollins families would get together there every year at noon. Johnny made a big pot of chili mostly by himself—I know he made it because I went to the store with him to buy the beans, and helped chop the meat and peppers. The chili cooked all day, the next morning we brought it with us to Mr. Rollins' house in a big pot. John Rollins, for his part, would make black-eyed peas and cornbread cooked in a skillet. Boy, we had a hell of a lunch. The rest of the day was spent swimming and relaxing at the Rollins' estate.

One other thing that I almost forgot about was that on the wall going up the staircase at Cinnamon Hill there was a very large mounted crocodile hide. When I inquired about it, John told me the story of how he was out one night on a boat with his friend Ross Kananga when they spotted movement in the water. It turned out to be a rouge crocodile that had been ravaging the area. When they shined a spotlight in the water, two green eyes were staring back at them.

Johnny took out a rifle and with one shot thought he killed it, however when they got closer to the croc it was still moving and Ross ended its misery with three shots from his pistol. That croc now graced the staircase wall. Johnny said his friend had started a crocodile farm a half-hour drive north on the way toward Ochos Rios, and the next day Johnny drove Cindy, Tiffany and myself to this croc farm, which had been in the

The Croc That Didn't Get Away

James Bond movie *Live and Let Die*, where Roger Moore walks across the backs of crocodiles to escape. This was the first time I had seen live crocs up close pretty scary I tell you. After spending an hour or so looking at reptiles we headed back, but not before stopping to talk to some native women who were walking along the road carrying fresh fruit on their heads. Right away they recognized John, Mr. Cash, Mr. Cash and of course he bought a week's supply of bananas and mangos from them.

Well all good things must come to an end. My flight was to leave the next morning at seven, which meant that I had to leave around five to get to the airport on time. Johnny arranged for his security chief to drive me. That night we said our goodbyes and went to bed. When I got up at 4:45 a.m., Johnny was waiting downstairs with a pot of coffee just to make sure that I was up on time and confirm that the driver showed up. We hugged goodbye but not before he gave me a small bag with two gifts inside. One was a first edition United States Postage Stamp depicting the Carter Family, on a June Carter Cash envelope, and the other was a commemorative Case "Moby Dick" pocketknife, individually scrimshawed and numbered. What could I say, but thank you so much, my friend, for making this the most memorable New Year's ever. The year was now 1994, and that vacation was just the recharge I needed.

Chapter 18 The All-Star Tribute

This is a tale of the last time Johnny Cash, and Marshall Grant, WS Holland and Bob Wootton (The Tennessee Three) ever performed together, and how it all came about .The setting was the Hammerstein Ballroom, located in New York City on 34th Street near 8th Avenue, and the show was called "An All-Star Tribute to Johnny Cash." The date: April 6th, 1999. Now for a little background.

W.S. "Fluke" Holland and John Carter

When Johnny first started out in the music business, he formed a group known as Johnny Cash and the Tennessee Two, with Marshall Grant on bass, and Luther Perkins on guitar. Several years later a drummer was added, W. S. "Fluke" Holland, and soon after the name was changed to Johnny Cash and the Tennessee Three.

Sadly on August 5 1968, Luther Perkins perished in a fire at his home, and he was eventually replaced by Bob Wootton, who continued as Johnny's guitar player until John's death. In February of 1980, while he was on one of his binges, and out of the clear blue sky, Johnny Cash fired his longtime friend and bass player Marshall Grant. This caused a lot of bad blood between them, and forced Marshall to file a lawsuit, which was eventually settled out of court. Marshall in his book *I Was There When It Happened: My Life with Johnny Cash* goes into great detail of the events that led up to his termination. I think as time went by, Johnny regretted the whole incident and it weighed heavily on his mind. They finally made up after the suit was settled around 1997. This was around the time when Johnny started to get ill.

June told me that whenever Marshall, who lived in Hernando, Mississippi, was in town; he would always stop over to spend time with John. Well, with that background April 6, 1999, was the night of taping the All Star Tribute to Johnny Cash and it was the first time that Johnny Cash and The Tennessee Three performed together in 19 years. Sadly, it would also be their last time. It was fabulous to see them all on stage again, and to see Marshall smiling as he played that big upright bass—man, he slapped that thing, just like he did for Sam Phillips 43 years earlier at Sun Records. He didn't miss a beat.

The show was performed live for rebroadcast as a TNT Special the next week. June had called me the week before to make sure that I contacted Lou Robin, John's manager, for tickets and backstage passes, which I did. On the day of the show my son

Henry Jr. drove me into the city around noon. We parked a block away from the venue, and once we went into the ballroom, I immediately hooked up with my friend Bob Wootton and spent the entire balance of the day with him, seeing old friends again and watching the rehearsals. I had some precious moments with Marshall Grant who I had known since 1976 but had not seen in many years. I watched as he put tape on his fingers to protect them, as the calluses had long since disappeared.

Brother Bob and I

It was nice to see everybody again from the Johnny Cash show: WS Holland, Earl Poole Ball, John Carter, Marty Stuart, Bob Wootton, Peggy Knight, Jay Dauro, Kent Elliot, Larry Johnson, Brian Farmer and the rest of his sound crew. Folks, if you are a Johnny Cash fan, it doesn't get any bigger than this show. Every performer had to wear black and sing a Johnny Cash song. The show was hosted by actor Jon Voight, and here's a list of who was there and what they sang:

Brooks and Dunn: *"Ghost Riders in the Sky"*
Gospel group The Fairfield Four: *"Belshazzer,"*
Lyle Lovett: *"Tennessee Flat Top Box"*
Wyclef Jean: *"Delia's Gone"*
Willie Nelson and Sheryl Crow: *"Jackson"*;
Chris Isaak: *"I Guess Things Happen That Way"*
The Mavericks: "Get Rhythm" and *"Man in Black"*
Willie Nelson: *"I Still Miss Someone"*
Willie and Kris Kristofferson: *"Big River"*

June Carter Cash with Marty Stuart: *"Ring of Fire"*
U2: *"Don't Take Your Guns to Town"*
Kris Kristofferson, with a member of the United States Marine Corp: *"Ballad of IraHayes"*
Trisha Yearwood and Kris: *"Sunday Morning Coming Down"*
Bruce Springsteen: *"Give My Love to Rose"*
Emmylou Harris, Sheryl Crow and Mary Chapin Carpenter: *"Flesh and Blood"*
Dave Matthews: *"The Long Black Veil"*
Bob Dylan: *"Train Of Love"*

And the grand finale (and what a finale it was!): actor Tim Robbins standing on the left-hand corner of the blackened stage with a spotlight shining only on him, reading the liner notes from the album *Live at Folsom Prison,* which were written by Johnny which deals with the lonely life and despair of a prisoner behind bars. As he finished, a dim spotlight turned to center stage as the backlights gradually came on. A shadow of a large man appeared with his back to the audience, his guitar slung over his shoulder. He slowly turned around, and as the spotlight intensified, that familiar deep voice said, "Hello, I'm Johnny Cash."

Of course, the crowd went wild. He licked his fingers, got his guitar pick from his pocket, then Bob Wootton, wearing his trademark black cowboy hat, and as he had done so many times in the past kicked off "Folsom Prison Blues." Johnny was backed up by John Carter Cash on rhythm guitar, Marty Stuart on guitar, Earl Poole Ball on piano, Bob Wootton on lead guitar, Marshall Grant on upright bass, and WS Holland on drums.

Even though Johnny's voice was weakened by then, as he sang his signature song, the audience sang along with him. He received several standing ovations and had to gesture with his hands to quiet down the crowd. You can just picture Johnny Cash standing tall with his guitar slung over his back, as he then thanked all those who contributed to his success, from Sam Phillips at Sun Records, to Don Law, his record producer at Columbia Records. With a special thanks to Marshall Grant, he then introduced the entire band, and next he told Willie that he was going to get the bus warmed up because he was ready to hit the road again.

With Kris

Johnny now moved closer to the audience as he threaded a piece of paper through his guitar strings (to imitate the sound of a snare drum because on the original recording of " I Walk the Line "he had no drummer) and he said, "I remember it so well. It started like this." Johnny started playing his guitar using a matchbook cover instead of guitar pick to achieve that original snare drum sound, and does this for a while without any backup music, alone on the front of the stage. Then all of a sudden it exploded.

Bob Wootton hit that familiar boom-chic-a-boom sound of "I Walk the Line," and as Johnny started singing, the entire full band came on. By the time he got through the second verse, Johnny had been joined on stage, first by June then Rosanne, and the rest one by one until the entire cast was singing "I Walk the Line."

And that was the single most amazing show I ever attended. Thank you, Johnny Cash, for coming into my life.

Valerie June Carter Cash

June 23, 1929 – May 15, 2003

Chapter 19
In Lieu of Donations, Please Send Flowers

Goodbye To June Carter Cash

July of 2002 was the last time I ever saw Johnny and June together. I was attending a NAMM (National Association of Music Merchants) trade show being held in Nashville, as the Vaccaro Guitar Company was displaying their new line of electric guitars and basses for the benefit of music dealers and distributors in North America. The show lasted four days, Thursday through Sunday. I had not seen Johnny for a couple of years, as his health was declining and he did not do that much traveling. It was only on a rare occasion that I would visit Nashville, and this trade show was one. I called the Cash home around noon on Saturday, and Peggy Knight picked up the phone. Peggy was like a Girl Friday, as she would do anything that John or June needed her to do. I asked her if John felt well enough for a couple of visitors, and she said, "For you, absolutely, come on over."

When I and a few people from my company arrived after our trade show that night, June opened the door and let us in, we hugged and then kissed each other on the cheek. They had just finished supper and John was watching TV in his easy chair in the living room. I glanced over at the TV to see what show he was watching; it was The Grand Ole Opry. John got up and we also hugged each other, and then I introduced the other folks that had come with me. John, although obviously not feeling that great, took everyone for a tour of his magnificent home, and took pride in explaining what artists had visited them in the past and what songs had been sung for the first time here in their living room.

It was a custom after the Johnny Cash Shows at the Ryman Auditorium to invite all the guests back to their home and sit around the octagonal great room overlooking Old Hickory Lake, then pass the guitar around for everyone to pick and sing. June called it a "guitar pull," and she claimed it was a good way to bond with their fellow musicians and to thank them for appearing on the Johnny Cash Show. One such night, John told me that Joni Mitchell sang "Both Sides Now," Bob Dylan unveiled "Lay Lady Lay" while Kris Kristofferson did "Me and Bobby McGee," all for the first time at the Old Hickory Lake house. Other artists that participated in these guitar pulls were Waylon Jennings, Graham Nash, Billy Joe Shaver, Rodney Crowell, the Statler Brothers and just anybody who wanted to come over.

June made some coffee and offered us some pastry. While we were all gathered in the living room, Paul Unkert, who was the plant manager at the Vaccaro Guitar Company, said, "Mr. Cash, how long have you and Henry known each other?" Johnny paused a moment, then said, "I think it's been at least thirty years or more. We were in several businesses together, right Henry?"

I nodded yes.

"Let's see, we were in the guitar business, right Henry?"

I nodded yes again.

"We were in the hotel business?"

Another nod yes.

"And I guess you could say we were even in the fishing business, right Henry?" he said, referring to all our trips to Bimini.

We laughed, and after a short period of reminiscing, I could sense that they were both getting tired, so I rounded up our group and said we better be leaving. June escorted us outside, where we all took a group photo. Sadly that was the last time I ever saw the wonderful June Carter Cash.

The Vaccaro Guitar Crew Meeting with June

June was having some heart problems, so she decided on elective surgery to replace a heart valve. The surgery was performed at Baptist Hospital in Nashville, and she came through with flying colors. However, a day later a blood clot was dislodged and went to her brain; in essence she was brain dead and put on life support. Johnny gathered his family around and they made the difficult decision to remove her from life support, on May 15, 2003.

The obituary in the *Tennessean*, beside listing the details of the funeral arrangements and surviving family members, read "In lieu of donations, please send flowers." Well there were more flowers at that funeral home than I have ever seen anywhere, except maybe at a flower show. Flowers came from all over the world, from England, Australia and Jamaica, just to name a few. I arrived in Nashville on Friday, May 16, rented a car and drove to Hendersonville. I was traveling with my son-in-law, Mark Bahary, as I did not want to travel alone.

We checked into a hotel that Lou Robin recommended not far from the Baptist Church where the service was to be held, a mile or so from the funeral home. Mark and I visited the funeral home on both Friday and Saturday nights. It was so sad to see John in a wheelchair being pushed by Peggy Knight; he looked so frail. I went over to pay my condolences, and he could hardly raise his hand to shake. Right away I could sense that he would soon follow June.

Some of the folks that I recognized at the funeral home were Carlene, Tom T. Hall, Hank Jr., Jane Seymour, Merle Kilgore, Ralph Emery, Larry Gatlin, Sheryl Crow, and Wynonna Judd. Kris, Jerry Hensley, Jack Shaw, Kathy, Cindy, Rosanne, Rosie, John Carter, Jimmy Title, Earl

Ball, Tommy Cash, Rodney Crowell, The Statler Brothers, Bob Wootton, WS Holland, and former Vice President Al Gore.

The service at the Baptist Church was something very special, as it was a real celebration of June's life. It started with Larry Gatlin and the Gatlin Brothers singing "Help Me" followed by Pastor Glen Weekly's remarks. Emmylou Harris then sang "Angel Band," Reverend Courtney Wilson spoke about June's life and how she inspired people, and mentioned the times she would attend church and bring John with her. Rosanne told a very beautiful story about how one day while June was visiting her in her New York home when the phone rang and June picked it up and carried on a long conversation with someone on the other end. Rosanne said they must have spoken for over a half hour, and when June hung up she told Rosanne what a wonderful lady that was. "Who was it?" Rosanne asked. "I don't know; she dialed you by mistake." And that was June, carrying on a long conversation with someone she didn't even know, and probably making the stranger feel as if they were lifelong friends.

Now it was time for the Oak Ridge Boys to sing,

"Loving God, Loving Each Other" followed by Sheryl Crow and "The Sea of Galilee." Next came a long procession of family and friends speaking about this beautiful lady. Laura Cash, John Carter's wife played and sang "How Great Thou Art," and to close the services, June's family from Virginia—Joe Carter, Janette Carter, Lorrie Bennett, and Dale Jett—all sang, and were joined by all the others in "Anchored in Love." And the next thing I knew it was all over, as I said goodbye to this beautiful woman, Valerie June Carter Cash, in the spring of 2003.

Chapter 20
Goodbye To The Man in Black

I knew that after seeing John at June's funeral on May 18, 2003 that he would not last too long, June was to John what Nancy was to President Reagan, and Gracie was to George Allen: inseparable, partners for life. By this time all the health problems and accidents in his life had caught up to him. Johnny was in a wheelchair, looking very frail. His eyesight was going and he had trouble breathing, but that voice, although scratchy and thin, was still there. Last year, meaning in 2011, when I saw John Carter, he told me that a few days after June's funeral his dad was already back recording, as that's all he knew.

But how about a little side story, first, before we get to the sad part. While in Bimini on one of our fishing trips some eighteen years earlier, Johnny and I were walking alone down the King's Highway, after having dinner at a place called the Red Lion. We were heading back to the Big Game Club when we heard the sound of native music and singing coming from some local club. Out of the clear blue sky, Johnny turned to me and said, "Henry, you know how I want to die? I want to die on stage playing music with my band. That's what I love; that's my life." I don't know what brought that comment on, and he never mentioned anything like that again.

I got the first word of Johnny's death from a newsbreak on a TV show. I'd been expecting it, but it was still a shock. Lou Robin, John's manager (Lou would always call him JR, which was his real first name, as it was Sam Phillips that named him Johnny) called the next day to give me the funeral arrangements. We talked about how we could not believe that this incredible chapter in both our lives was now over.

I called my friend Joe Simmons, and asked him if he wanted to go to the funeral with me, for Joe had befriended John and attended many shows with me. He immediately said yes, and I told him that I would make the plane reservations, and "By the way, bring along your pipes." I

My friend Joe Simmons and Johnny

was referring to his bagpipes, as Joe was the official piper for Governor James McGreevy of New Jersey. He said what for? Just bring them anyway. Joe packed his pipes and kilts in his suitcase. Lou had gotten us reservations at the Holiday Inn right down the street from the Baptist church where the services were to be held, and close to the funeral home and cemetery.

It's strange how things happen almost as if God's hand is guiding our every move. Joe and I had no sooner checked into the hotel than we saw Lou Robin and his wife Karen in the lobby. I introduced them to my friend Joe, and told him that Joe, who was the official bagpiper for the governor of New Jersey, would love to play bagpipes at the funeral. Joe was kind of embarrassed, as he was unaware that I was going to make such a request. Lou replied that it sounded great, but needed to first clear it with Rosanne. Sure enough, Lou knocked on our door a few minutes later and said the family would love it, as Rosanne said the Cash's were of Scottish descent. Thus, my little scheme worked, and here my friend Joe Simmons, from a tiny town in New Jersey called Ocean Grove, would be playing his pipes for the biggest show of them all.

There was a private viewing for family and friends at the Hendersonville Funeral Home in Hendersonville, Tennessee on Sunday, September 14, 2003. Joe Simmons and I spent the afternoon and evening there, and I fortunately had the chance to get reacquainted with old friends. Thank God I wrote down the names of those attending, so some nine years later as I write this book I can share those names with you. There not in any order but here they are: Bob Lewin, Jack Hale, Jr., Jay Dauro, Larry Johnson, Brian Farmer, Kent Elliot, Braxton Dixon, The Statler Brothers, Tom T. Hall, Kris Kristofferson, Bobby Bare, Rosanne, Cindy, Tara, Kathy, John Carter, and their spouses, Tiffany Lowe and all the other grandchildren, Vice President Al Gore, W.S. Holland, Marshall Grant, Bob Wootton, Earl Poole Ball, Larry Gatlin, Roger Morton, Wirehead, Peggy Knight, Lou and Karen Robin, Ralph Emery, Johnny Western, Cowboy Jack Clement,

Marty Stuart, Connie Smith, Emmylou Harris, Jimmy Title, Rodney Crowell, Merle Kilgore, Tommy Cash, Reba, Kelly Hancock, Hank Williams, Jr., Sheryl Crow, Kid Rock, Jeannie C. Riley, Hugh Waddell, Jane Seymour, James Keach, Michele Rollins, Ted Rollins, Rosemarie Edelman, Jack Shaw, George Hamilton IV, George Jones, Rick Rubin, Kix Brooks, The Gatlin Brothers, Ronnie and Jeanine Dunn, Luther Perkins' wife, Brian Ahern, John Mellencamp, Billy Walker, The Whites, Ricky Skaggs, The Oak Ridge Boys, Randy Scruggs, John Leventhal, and a bunch of other folks I'm sure that I inadvertently left out.

And soon came Monday, September 15, 2003, a day that I want to forget in so many ways, yet in others I want it to be always etched in my memory. That morning, Joe and I got up around seven, cleaned up, and went downstairs for breakfast, where we bumped into Bob Wootton sitting at a table alongside WS Holland and his wife. We joined them, and naturally the small talk was about Johnny and the great trip through life they'd had with him, about that wonderful ride they'd been on for so many years, and how they experienced places and events that they never in their wildest dreams would have ever imagined, considering the humble backgrounds that they both came from. For Joe and me it was a nice breakfast, just to relive those stories first-hand, told by the people who were there and made history with the Man in Black.

After breakfast we tried to plan our day around the funeral, which was scheduled at 12 o'clock. We drove to the funeral home and the adjacent cemetery, timed the drive, and then went back to the hotel to dress for the service. The plan was to leave the hotel around 11:15, drive to the church, and park in a location where we could get

Bob Wootton, W.S. Holland and His Wife Joyce at Breakfast the Morning of Johnny's Funeral. Lou Robin standing in the background.

out fast and beat the funeral procession to the cemetery. Our plan was on schedule.

We changed clothes back at the hotel, Joe put on his kilt and we then got in the car as I drove to the church, parked in a perfect location and informed the police officer that we had to leave early to get to the cemetery before the procession. Joe and I waited for the church doors to open and mingled with some of the folks outside. I recall talking at length to Barbara Mandrell and Ralph Emery. Then the doors opened and we made a beeline for seats that would afford us easy access to leave without disturbing anyone during the service. We selected our seats and who sits next to Joe, but none other than country legend George Hamilton IV. George was known as the international ambassador of country music, and I believe that he too had some Scottish blood in him. They chatted and soon George inquired why Joe was dressed in a kilt. We'd planned on leaving early so as to position Joe at the cemetery, ready to play as they walked the casket from the hearse to the gravesite.

The church service itself seemed like a divine production with God's hand in every part of it. The service opened with a hymn sung by the Fisk Jubilee Singers, whom Johnny had loved. This was followed by a prayer from Reverend Courtney Wilson.

Dr. Franklin Graham, the son of Billy Graham delivered a beautiful message, and passed on words of wisdom from his father who was ill and at home. Emmylou Harris then sang a gospel song in that beautiful voice of hers. There were three eulogies delivered. The first from Lou Robin, Johnny's manager and his close friend and advisor for over thirty years. And all those years without a signed contract, just the man's word, which was good enough for Lou, who spoke of those travels through life and what a great man Johnny was to work for.

Cowboy Jack Clement was Johnny's first ever record producer when he worked for Sam Phillips at Sun Records way back in the beginning in 1955, and so Jack talked about those days. The final eulogy was delivered by Johnny's longtime friend Kris Kristofferson, as only he could do in his eloquent manner. Kris was in tears with his voice cracking, recalling how he and John first met, and confessing how he'd even taken a job as a janitor at Columbia Records in Nashville just to get a chance to meet and see him. Kris talked about the time he "borrowed" a helicopter from the Army, without their permission of course and flew it over to Johnny's house in Hendersonville, unannounced, and landed it on the side lawn, just to deliver some tapes of songs he had written to the man himself. As it turned out, one of those songs was called "Sunday Morning Coming Down," which Johnny later recorded, and which became a number-one hit.

Kris also recalled how Johnny had once stood up to an executive at the ABC television network that produced The Johnny Cash Show when the producer wanted Johnny to alter the lyrics of "Sunday Morning Coming Down" before singing it on the show. They wanted the lyrics "I'm wishing lord that I was stoned," changed to "I'm wishing lord that I was home." Johnny refused and said I will do the song the way Kris wrote it, and he did. Kris ended his comments by stating that the next face to adorn Mt. Rushmore should be that of this "Holy Warrior," John R. Cash.

As the church service started to wind down Larry Gatlin took center altar and along with members of the Cash family sang "Angel Band." That was followed by a benediction by Dr. Franklin Graham, Reverend Courtney Wilson and Brother Glenn Weekly. As the Fisk Jubilee Singers began the closing song, Joe Simmons and I made our way to the side door and left; we quickly got the car and headed to the cemetery. The drive took approximately ten minutes.

Once at the cemetery, we parked the car out of the way, and walked over to the gravesite to scope out where Joe might play. I spotted an evergreen tree about 50 feet from Johnny's grave plot. We jointly decided that would be the perfect place for Joe to place himself until he was ready. By now the entire funeral procession had reached the cemetery. There was a large green canopy covering the grave itself, and artificial grass spread on the ground beneath the canopy. Folding chairs were set up on this artificial grass, with about 50 chairs for family members and standing room for the rest. John Carter and his sisters Carlene, Rosie, Rosanne, Kathy, Cindy and Tara sat in the front row with Johnny's brother Tommy and his sisters behind them.

The pallbearers carried the casket from the hearse and set it on an aluminum frame directly over the grave. While the casket was being moved from the hearse, Joe Simmons, dressed in his full Scottish kilt uniform complete with high socks and all, stood off to the side and played, "When the Battle's Over." Joe started playing as the casket was being moved and stopped when it reached the gravesite. He then did an about face, and marched away in plain sight to the evergreen tree, and stood at attention as the service proceeded.

Dr. Franklin Graham conducted the graveside service, and as he was saying the final prayer, with the casket being prepared for lowering into the ground, the undertaker gave Joe a hand signal to start playing "Amazing Grace." The song begins to resonate throughout the cemetery, leaving people spellbound. When it finished, Joe marched towards the grave playing "The Minstrel Boy," stopped, saluted,

My Friend Joe Simmons Playing the Bagpipes at Johnny's Funeral

and slowly marched away so that the tune would also fade away as people were paying their last respects. You could hear a pin drop. And in a few minutes it was all over.

Rosanne and John Carter went out of their way to thank Joe later, saying that their father would have been proud. Folks, I know that this happened, for I was there on that sad day,

September 15, 2003, as I had the highest honor of being an honorary pallbearer for my beloved friend, John R. Cash.

CASH

February 26, 1932 – September 12, 2003

Honorary Pallbearers:

Rodney Crowell	Michelle Rollins
Walter Eschenbach	Rick Rubin
David Ferguson	Fred Schwoebel
Marshall Grant	Bob Sullivan
John Leventhal	Jimmy Tittle
Luke Lewis	Henry Vaccaro
Eddie Panetta	Wayne Womack
Lou Robin	Harry Yates
Luther Fleaner	Joe Garrett
Willie Nelson	Kris Kristofferson

Joe Carter

Tommy Cash

Pallbearers:

Tony Bisceglia	Ted Rollins
Thomas Coggins	John Jackson Routh
Larry Gatlin	Randy Scruggs
Michael Rollins	Marty Stuart

Dustin Tittle

THE FAMILY OF
JOHNNY CASH
INVITES YOU TO JOIN THEM IN
A MEMORIAL TRIBUTE

MONDAY, NOVEMBER 10, 2003
7:30PM
RYMAN AUDITORIUM
NASHVILLE, TENNESSEE

MAIN FLOOR

SECTION MF-6   ROW L   SEAT 1

Chapter 21
The Memorial
Tribute
in Nashville
Tennessee

The date was November 10, 2003. The Place the Ryman Auditorium. The event the Johnny Cash Memorial Tribute. Folks, I was one of the privileged few to receive four tickets as well as backstage passes for this monumental event, thanks to my longtime friend and Johnny's manager, Lou Robin. Lou, through thick and thin, was always there for Johnny, and anytime I wanted anything he was there for me as well. I planned to take my friend Joe Simmons, and my office manager Jennifer Peters and her fiancé, Van.

We all flew together from Newark to Nashville and stayed at a Holiday Inn on Broadway within walking distance of the Ryman. Since we arrived two days before the show, it gave us time to explore Nashville and visit the Country Music Hall of Fame. The nights were great, as we hit one honky-tonk after another, starting with the famed Tootsie's Orchid Lounge, made famous by the likes of Willie Nelson and Kris Kristofferson. The back doors lead to the mother church of country music, the Ryman Auditorium.

The Memorial Tribute was set for Monday night, which meant rehearsals on Sunday and Monday during the daytime. As we all had backstage passes, we were permitted into the rehearsals, which sometimes can be as good as or better than the show. Lou provided us with great seats, as usual, in the fifth row center stage alongside the family. There were but a handful of people at the rehearsals, so we had plenty of time to chat with everyone, including the performers, who would come down from the stage and sit in the seats near us, just for a break. This gave me the opportunity to sit and chat with Hank Jr. I knew he was a history buff, so we shared stories of

WWII battles. He told me that both he and John were students of the Civil War but he was also into WWII, as a neighbor of his had landed in France on D-day. As a hobby, I've sometimes traveled to WWII battlefield sites, including a reenactment of the landings on Guadalcanal in the Solomon Islands.

Marshall Grant then joined us. A few minutes later, in walked Janine Dunn, Ronnie Dunn's wife of Brooks and Dunn fame, with some of her friends. I had previously met her at John Carter's wedding, and she and the Cash's were the closest of friends, so much so that when she and Ronnie first got married, Johnny let them stay in his log cabin at the game preserve until they could get on their feet. They never forgot that.

The rehearsals were informative. One of the things I found out was how powerful Hank Jr.'s voice was; he didn't even need a mike. After that event, I now clearly understand the reason for a sound check at each venue; it adjusts the amplification for each individual artist, and their ranges can vary greatly. Also at the rehearsals, you can watch the interactions of the artists, some whom have never sung with each other before. In between the Monday daytime rehearsal and the actual start of the show, I had the opportunity to go aboard Hank Jr.'s tour bus, which was parked alongside the Ryman. He was on the bus with Kid Rock, whom I knew as my Vaccaro Guitar Company had made two custom guitars for him, one hand painted with an American flag, the other with a Confederate flag. I only stayed a few minutes, as I wanted to eat before the show. Later, I found out that after the show ol' Hank and Kid Rock, who were apparently feeling no pain, and put on their own show at Tootsie's Orchid Lounge.

The inside CD Artwork for Kid Rocks History of Rock Featuring Kid Rock's Custom Vaccaro Guitars

Well, it was time for the last show to go on, and go on it did. Tim Robbins was the Master of Ceremonies, and the Who's Who of Country Music Royalty were the performers: Brooks and Dunn, Carlene Carter, Laura Cash, Rosanne Cash, Jack Clement, Sheryl Crow, Rodney Crowell, Steve Earle, the Fisk Jubilee Singers, Larry Gatlin, George Jones, Kid Rock, Kris Kristofferson, John Mellencamp, Willie Nelson, Randy Scruggs, Marty Stuart, Jimmy Tittle, Travis Tritt, Johnny Western, and Hank Williams Jr.

A couple of things disappointed me. One was that neither Bob Wootton nor W.S. Holland was on stage playing; these guys along with Marshall Grant were the last of the Tennessee Three, yet they did not perform. The other thing that I was not too fond of was the way Travis Tritt interpreted Johnny's song "I Walk the Line," nor was I crazy about John Mellencamp's version of "Hey, Porter." Those versions just seemed a little out of sync.

What I think I remember most about this show were the personal stories that artists told about Johnny. Hank Jr. told about the time he fell down a mountain and his face was ripped open. He lost one eye and was in a coma, and when he awoke several days later in the hospital, Johnny and June (who was Hank Jr.'s godmother) were standing over him. Ronnie Dunn almost broke down as he talked about the generosity of both Johnny and June, when in 1999, after he'd just moved to Nashville, John gave him one of his custom made stage coats to wear.

Hank Jr. and Kid Rock

Marshall Grant then came on stage and spent about twenty minutes talking about how it all started. Marshall had to compose himself when he started talking about how he and John first met. He and Luther Perkins were auto mechanics at a DeSoto-Plymouth dealership in Memphis, and Roy Cash, John's older brother, also worked there. According to Marshall, some evenings, he and Luther would pick a little guitar together after work. Roy heard about it and mentioned that he had a brother who had just gotten out of the Air Force, someone who also picked and sang and was on his way to Memphis. Several days later, Marshall and Luther were then introduced to J.R. Cash. John had an old cheap guitar that he'd bought in Germany for $5.

The One and Only Marshall Grant

Luther had a pretty good one, and Marshall had a Martin guitar. The first thing they learned was an old gospel song, with Marshall and Johnny doing the singing and all three playing rhythm.

They soon heard of a kid named Elvis Presley who had a hit record over at Sun Studios, not too far from the DeSoto dealership. They decided that they wanted to make a record but knew that they needed better instruments, as all they had between them were three acoustic guitars. Luther had a friend who lent him an old beat-up Fender telecaster; Marshall purchased a very used upright bass for $25 dollars (that he didn't even know how to tune) and gave John his Martin guitar to replace the one from Germany. According to Marshall, "After work one day we all went to Sun Studios on Union Avenue. We just walked in, no appointment, and told the owner Sam Phillips that we wanted to make a record. Into the studio we went, and our very first song was a gospel song "I Was There When It Happened, So I Guess I Ought To Know."

Sam cut in and said "Grant, slap that bass harder", and as we did another take, Sam, came in from the control room with a smile and said, 'Boys I can't sell gospel music but there is something about you guys that I like. If you can come up with an original song, bring it in.' The very next week John stopped by the DeSoto agency and told us he had this song 'Hey Porter' that he wrote, and so we started to learn the song. We practiced, practiced, and practiced till we got it right. We developed this very simple boom-chic a-boom sound by accident, because that's all we knew.

"People thought we worked years to develop that sound, but truth is we worked hard to get rid of it. Now it's back to see Sam Phillips again. We played 'Hey Porter' and Sam recorded it, but he said 'I need another song for the flip side.' The very next week John showed up with a poem, 'Cry, Cry, Cry,' and we practiced until we made it into a song. We went *back* to Sun and recorded that one. Sam said, 'I like it, and I like it a lot.' This was in May 1955. Sam released it, and although we didn't know it yet, we just made musical history. Here we were two mechanics and an appliance salesman [Johnny had taken a job selling appliances door to door]. We certainly were not musicians but we just made a record." At this point, Marshall paused and shook his head, and all of us in the audience were transfixed by this simple story that turned into a tale of greatness. Folks, you know the rest of the story.

Chapter 22

Special Friends That I Met with Johnny

Over a thirty-year period of being around or with Johnny Cash and June Carter Cash, I have come to know and meet many, many friends of theirs, some who were very famous and some not-so famous, but all good, down-to-earth people just the same. I think one of Johnny's closest friends outside of the music business was John Rollins, who came from humble beginnings to become a very successful businessman and politician. John Rollins, who would later become Johnny's neighbor down in Jamaica, was born in 1916 in the tiny town of Keith, Georgia, and he would walk nine miles a day just to attend a one-room school. His father became ill, and at age twelve, John Rollins started selling anything he could door-to-door to help support the family.

He left the farm to move to Philadelphia and then to Lewes, Delaware. According to Johnny, there John Rollins started selling used cars. He had very little money so he and his brother would sleep in the car at night, and after they sold the car they now had enough money to buy two cars, so now at night each brother had his own private back seat to sleep in. They would read the obituary daily, and when someone of Irish descent would pass away they would get dressed and go to the wake and of course gratefully partake in the food served afterwards. John Rollins had a great mind for business even then, and soon opened a Ford dealership in Delaware, then in Virginia and Maryland. He pioneered auto- and truck-leasing.

By the time that Johnny Cash introduced me to him, John Rollins owned Rollins Leasing Co., Matlack Truck Lines (the nation's largest bulk carrier), Orkin Pest Control, Rollins Broadcasting Co., Dover Motorsports, Rollins Environmental Co. and 75 % of all the billboards in Mexico. All in all, he formed nine public companies that traded on the NYSE. As a politician, he was elected Lt. Governor of Delaware and was the largest private landowner in Jamaica, even after he sold Cinnamon Hill to Johnny.

147

Johnny also told me how powerful Mr. Rollins was politically. When it was discovered that squatters had taken over large amounts of his property in Jamaica, he contacted the Jamaican government, who refused to remove them. But it seems that ol' John had a friend in the White House named Richard Nixon, who threatened to cut off all foreign aid to Jamaica until the squatters left Mr. Rollins' property. I became very friendly with John Rollins, his third wife Michele, a former Miss USA, and their son Ted, who sometimes played guitar on Johnny's shows.

Goldie Adcock, Louis B. Robin, his wife Karen and Myself

Another person I met and became close friends with was John's promoter and later his personal manager, Mr. Lou Robin. Lou is a man of impeccable character, and maybe that's why he worked for John for over 30 years just on a handshake. Lou was always there for John and handled every situation, good or bad, with class and distinction. John's family has so much respect for him that even nine years after Johnny's death; Lou continues to handle the estate in all dealings with anything regarding the exploitation of the Johnny Cash brand.

Lou started his promotions company in 1957, and before promoting the Johnny Cash Show he was instrumental in developing the early careers of The Kingston Trio, The Carpenters, Simon and Garfunkel, Steve Martin and others. Lou's long arm reached all the way to Hawaii, where he promoted and became best friends with Don Ho. Lou has been a great friend to me, and helped me out anytime I needed anything, from tickets to the Grammy Legends Show or to the front lawn of the Capitol for 4th of July celebration. He has even been instrumental in helping me with my Michael Jackson Collection. But that's another story for another book.

June, too, had many great friends that I met. One was Rosemary Edelman, the daughter of famed TV and movie producer Louis Edelman; she at one time shared a New York apartment with June. Rosemary, who lived in Hollywood, would sometimes visit June in Asbury Park at the Berkeley Carteret Hotel. I would see her and her sister Kate at various functions at Johnny and June's home in Tennessee, including weddings and parties. The last time I saw them was at John's funeral.

Another friend of June's was the actor Robert Duvall, whom June referred to as Bobby Duvall. They'd both studied acting together at the Actor's Studio in New York City and we met backstage at a concert in Anaheim, California. June also introduced me to Colonel Tom Parker at a reception held at The College of the Desert in California. On April 28, 1984 Johnny performed a concert there to thank the doctors who helped him while he was in the Betty Ford Clinic. June told me that the Colonel, as he liked to be called, once managed the Carter Family and at one point in time played drums on an Elvis Presley show.

John and June had another close friend named Bill Patch, who owned a coal mining operation in Welch, Oklahoma. Bill constructed a Cadillac car to match the car described in Johnny's song "One Piece at a Time" (as the song goes, this car is made up of pieces of a Cadillac car stolen over a period of years and assembled with odd mismatched pieces), and had it shipped to Hendersonville to give to John as a gift. They became close friends and Johnny did a benefit concert in Welch to help pay for a new civic center. A few years later, Bill Patch died of cancer and his wife Janine moved to Nashville. As I was single then, June tried to fix me up with Janine, whom she politely called Widow Patch. As it turned out, the widow, whom I never met until John Carter's wedding, was drop dead gorgeous, and she eventually married Ronnie Dunn of Brooks and Dunn fame. Oh, woe is me.

Without going into great detail, the following people were all introduced to me by Johnny or June: Billy Graham, Bob Wootton, Marshall Grant, W.S. Holland, Earl Poole Ball, Jerry Hensley, John Schneider, Marla Maples, Barbara Mandrell, Andy Griffith, Kris Kristofferson, Waylon Jennings, Willie Nelson, Jerry Lee Lewis, Bill and Shannon Miller, Carl Perkins, Hank Williams Jr, Merle Kilgore, Jon Voight, George Jones, Tammy Wynette, Hank Snow, Ernest Tubb, Gene Autry, Kix Brooks, Ronnie Dunn and his wife Janine, Peggy Knight, The Statler Brothers, Dick Asher, The Oak Ridge Boys, Bill Monroe, Vince Gill, John Prine, Steve Goodman, Rodney Crowell, James Whitmore, Tim Robbins, Hugh Waddell, Dave Dudley, Trisha Yearwood, Emmylou Harris, Jimmy Dean, Roy Acuff, Sheryl Crow, Marty Stuart, Connie Smith, Mary Chapin Carpenter, Lyle Lovett, Ralph Emery, Jane Seymour, Shooter Jennings, Jessi Colter, Jeannie C. Riley, Arthur Smith, John J. Hooker, Wyclef Jean, Larry Gatlin, Elton John, Brooke Shields, and her mom, Teri, as well as many others.

Whenever you were in the company of Johnny or June, they would always make sure that you felt comfortable and at ease, and welcome you as part of their extended family. They just had this way about them.

Willie

Larry Gattlin

John's Sister Joanne and her Husband

Connie Smith, Marty Stuart

CHAPTER 23

Will You Meet Me in Heaven Someday?

Those are words contained in the chorus of a song by John R. Cash, and those very words grace the back cover of his funeral program. I thought those words were the right way to end the final chapter in this book dedicated to his life, as I hope to meet him again someday in heaven.

Words are hard to come by now as I conclude my quest to memorialize in writing my 30-odd-year friendship with this incredible human being that God put on this earth for all people of all faiths to look up to. I really don't know how to end this final chapter, except to again emphasize the profound effect that this man had on my entire life, even now in 2012, some nine years after his death. Not one single day goes by that I don't think about him, or talk about him.

I happened to be on a WWII adventure tour to the island of Iwo Jima a couple of years ago, and we made a stop in Guam for several days prior to taking a charter flight to Iwo Jima. On two different occasions on this remote paradise in the middle of the Pacific Ocean, I heard

Johnny Cash songs, both on the TV and on the radio. And the same thing happened in Germany while walking down a street; the music I heard coming out of a small store was "I Walk the Line." I soon came to realize what an impact this man had, not only on my life, but also on the lives of fans and music lovers all over the world. He touched so many people, from royalty to the common folk. Just think: every single day, at any point in time, somebody, someplace in the world is listening to a Johnny Cash song.

Sometimes I close my eyes and search my memory back to picture the first time I shook his hand. Then I let my mind wander on, and try to reminisce as vividly as I can. I remember all those fabulous moments that we shared together, whether alone on a fishing boat, on a Learjet, on his tour bus, walking the streets of Bimini, or in the woods at his game preserve in Hendersonville Tennessee.

It was Johnny that our family turned to when it was discovered that my late sister Roe had an addiction problem. He not only helped us, but personally made the phone call to get her admitted to Cumberland Heights Treatment Center in Nashville Tennessee. Roe told me that one Sunday afternoon while she was in the main area of the women's center, in walked Johnny Cash with several bags full of clothes, and other personal sundry items that he'd purchased for her at a nearby Wal-Mart. He spent the next several hours talking to her and trying to lift her spirits. Roe came home six weeks later, out of the woods thanks in large part to Johnny.

On another trip together, we visited Palm Aire Spa in Pompano Beach, Florida. Johnny and June stayed with their close friends, John and Michele Rollins who were investors in the massive spa and hotel complex. I stayed along with my daughter Toni at the Spa Hotel. My daughter Toni at the time was coming out of a rocky marriage and she recalls Johnny taking long walks with her and spending the time to talk to and comfort her. These little things made him so special. He did not have to do that, but he did walk with and talked with people because he wanted to.

I can also remember those surprise phone calls out of the clear blue sky, like "Henry, June and I are in New York. We just got some tickets for a Broadway show, Will Rogers Follies, starring my friend Larry Gatlin. Would you and Henry Jr. like to meet us at the theater tonight at 7 o'clock?" Of course we went, and we not only saw the show, which was great, but went backstage afterwards to meet Larry and Marla Maples, who was also appearing in the show and at the time was married to Donald Trump. Speaking of Donald Trump, one night while Johnny was

playing at the Trump Marina Hotel in Atlantic City, New Jersey, I was in his dressing room when he received a note requesting him to announce from the stage that Donald Trump was in the audience, which would then cue a spotlight to find "The Donald."

Johnny was amused.

And then I remember way back in 1983, during the making of the movie *Murder in Coweta County,* we were on Johnny's bus, traveling from the movie set in

Griffin, Georgia to the Hyatt Regency Hotel in Atlanta. Bob Wootton and I were sitting in the front seating area near the driver, Roger Morton. June was in her area in the rear and Johnny was in his private compartment adjacent to us, going over some lines, when he called out, "Henry, come back here and talk to me.

"I got up and went back, and the first thing I did was to thank him for allowing me to spend this private time with him, and to travel on his bus. He re-

Johnny pictured with a bust I had commissioned of him

sponded, "You are here because I want you here. You don't know how many people want to ride this bus with me, but Henry, I want *you* here. Now take a look at these gems that I brought back from the Holy Land." He proceeded to empty a velvet bag of different gems on the table everything from rubies, emeralds, aquamarine, amethyst, onyx to topaz; there must have been over a hundred stones.

Johnny said, "Pick what you want."

I hesitated and did not know what to say.

"Well, then if you're not going to pick anything, I'll pick it for you." Johnny Cash then proceeded to pick two or three of each stone and put them in a smaller blue velvet bag with a gold tassel on it. He tied it up and said "It's yours." What could I say but, Thank you? I still have all those stones, in that same blue velvet bag.

Johnny was a man of peace and was firmly against all wars. *He once told me that there was no disagreement so great that it could not be settled if intelligent people would just sit down across from each other and talk.* As

much as he was against war, Johnny took his entire show to Vietnam to entertain our troops because he felt that was the right thing to do. Not only did he perform for the troops, but he and June visited the hospitals and took the time to speak to each and every wounded warrior. June took down the names, addresses and phone number of their folks at home, and she either called or wrote them to let them know that their loved ones were alright. On another occasion Johnny, June and the entire

show flew to Guantanamo Bay, Cuba for a day just to entertain the sailors stationed there.

I have to borrow my daughter's memory to go back again in time, to when June had written her book *From the Heart*. Our families were in Bimini for one of our fishing trips, and one day June stayed behind at the Big Game Club with Toni, my daughter. Toni tells that they were both sitting under a palm tree while June was writing her book on lined notebook paper, all in

longhand. After the book was published, it culminated in a book tour, and June took Toni and Peggy Knight with her on the first leg of this event. They left the Berkeley Carteret Hotel and went by limousine to Washington DC, where June appeared on the Larry King show with Toni acting as June's publicist. The book tour eventually ended up in Dallas.

Our families shared each other's happy events as well as those sad ones. I was invited to and attended John Carter's wedding on June 14, 1995, as well as that of John's youngest daughter, Tara, on June 13, 1991, and of June's daughter Rosie on May 22, 1988. I was also invited to John and June's Silver wedding anniversary party on March 2, 1993, and to John Carter's graduation on May 21, 1988. John and June attended my daughter Toni's wedding and June attended my surprise 45th birthday party. I attended the funeral of Johnny's dad, Mr. Ray Cash, and both Johnny and June attended my mother's funeral.

I particularly love to recall a visit with Johnny, June and John Carter one day in 1981. At their apartment on Central Park South, Johnny and I watched as our sons John Carter and Henry Jr crafted miniature helicopters out of paper and scissors in the living room. We then went over to the balcony leaned over and witnessed them float effortlessly away, floating away with the wind. Not knowing where they will end up.

John R Cash was a complex man. He was honest, strong-willed, and sometimes very quiet. He was a family man, spiritual, inspirational, and God-fearing. He was shy at times, largely peaceful, and above all, a real man with strong core values who stood by his convictions. I often think of those words of Kris Kristofferson, who said that Johnny Cash was really the father of our country and would love to one day find Johnny's face looking down from Mt. Rushmore with all those other great men, all those genuine American heroes.

When I think back from my youth to my old age Johnny Cash has been the sound track of my life and I was blessed to have also personally known him. He certainly did impact my life. He brought the best out in me. He restored my faith in God above and taught me what was really important in this life, your faith, your character, your family and friends and your compassion for your fellow man.

I suppose our friendship was destined to be, a divine intervention from above perhaps, maybe God had a message for me.

Well Dear Lord, Thank You for sending me one John R Cash to deliver it to me.

I Hope to see you in Heaven someday.